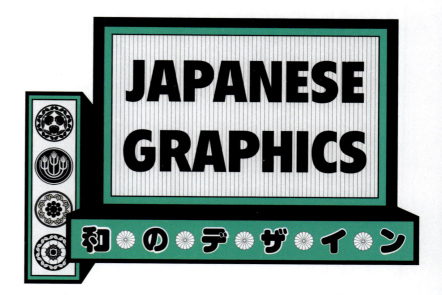

JAPANESE GRAPHICS
和●の●デ●ザ●イ●ン

SP

SendPoints

JAPANESE GRAPHICS

© 2019 SendPoints Publishing Co., Ltd.

EDITED & PUBLISHED BY SendPoints Publishing Co., Ltd.
PUBLISHER: Lin Gengli
PUBLISHING DIRECTOR: Lin Shijian
CHIEF EDITOR: Lin Shijian
EXECUTIVE EDITOR: Luo Yanmei   Look Hoi Yan
ART DIRECTOR: He Wanling
EXECUTIVE ART EDITOR: Look Hoi Yan
PROOFREADING: James N. Powell   Luo Yanmei

REGISTERED ADDRESS: Room 15A Block 9 Tsui Chuk Garden, Wong Tai Sin, Kowloon, Hong Kong
TEL: +852-35832323 / **FAX:** +852-35832448
OFFICE ADDRESS: 7F, 9th Anning Street, Jinshazhou, Baiyun District, Guangzhou, China
TEL: +86-20-89095121 / **FAX:** +86-20-89095206
BEIJING OFFICE: Room 107, Floor 1, Xiyingfang Alley, Ande Road, Dongcheng District, Beijing, China
TEL: +86-10-84139071 / **FAX:** +86-10-84139071
SHANGHAI OFFICE: Room 307, Building 1, Hong Qiang Creative, Zhabei District, Shanghai, China
TEL: +86-21-63523469 / **FAX:** +86-21-63523469

SALES MANAGER: Sissi
TEL: +86-20-81007895
EMAIL: overseas01@sendpoints.cn
WEBSITE: www.sendpoints.cn / www.spbooks.cn

ISBN 978-988-77572-1-4

SECOND PRINTING

Graphic Design in Japan

Masaaki Hiromura
| Art Director
| Hiromura Design Office

Masaaki was born in Aichi prefecture in 1954. He entered the Tanaka Design Office in 1977 and established the Hiromura Design Office in 1988. Awards include the JAGDA New Designer Award, the N.Y. ADC 9th International Annual Exhibition Silver Award, the CS Design Award (Decoration Category Gold Award), the SDA Diamond Award, the 15th CS Design Award (Sign Category Gold Award), the 2008 KU/KAN Award, the 2008 Mainichi Design Awards, the 44th SDA Awards (Grand Prize), the 2010 JCD Design Award (Grand Prize), the 2010 Good Design Award (Gold Prize), the 46th SDA Awards (Grand Prize) in 2012, the 47th SDA Awards (Grand Prize) in 2013, the 48th SDA Awards (Grand Prize) in 2014, among others.

Manufacturing-based Japanese design

How does Japanese graphic design differ from that of other countries?

Environmental currents deeply influence creativity: living, for instance, in a prosperous international era and cosmopolitan surroundings influences one's sense of nationality and belonging, providing a foundation for one's inventiveness.

In recent years, however, Japanese graphic design has been trying to bounce back from the downturn caused by economic decline. Back in the 1950s, along with the post-war reconstruction, Japanese graphic design ceased being seen merely as a side job for painters. Led by Yusaku Kamekura and Yoshio Hayakawa, the Japan Advertising Artists Club (JAAC) was established.

From 1951 to 1970, the JAAC Exhibition annually recruited and publically displayed a selection of excellent works. Ever since the JAAC Exhibition was held, professionals and amateurs in Japan who were longing to become "real designers" rushed to earn their chance for exposure. Those designers, who later became avant-garde in Japan, including Ikko Tanaka, Kazumasa Nagai, Tadanori Yokoo, and others, earned their fame from the exhibition. Later, in 1954, Yoko Kuwasawa, who was strongly influenced by the Bauhaus, founded the Kuwasawa Design School (KDS) in Tokyo, in order to promote and advance design education.

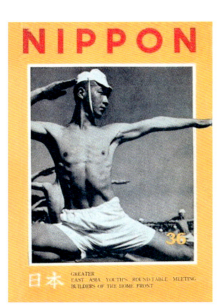

NIPPON,
published by Nippon Kobo design studio

In that era, Japan absorbed design styles mostly from Europe and America, including Bauhaus and Constructivism.

Before embracing American commercial styling in the early postwar years, an obvious divergence in design views had come about during wartime. So the Nippon Kobo design studio, joined by influential designers including Yusaku Kamekura, Takashi Kono, Yonosuke Natori, and Ken Domon, published its magazine *NIPPON* displaying the unique power of Japanese design of that era. With its bold images, the magazine pioneered the direction in which Japanese graphic design was heading: a simple, concise, yet uncompromisingly rich aesthetic. This idea, aligned with traditional bushido, flowed into modern times like a quiet current of groundwater.

Koetsu Honami and Sotatsu Tawaraya were co-founders of the Rinpa school, which transmitted its aesthetic from generation to generation. Then in the Edo period, Korin Ogata, Hoitsu Sakai, and many others consolidated this style. Although these works were only craftwork, they were consummately designed, even when judged from a contemporary viewpoint. These predecessors were actually acting out the responsibilities of a contemporary art director.

Irises, by Korin Ogata

Japanese sensibility springs from the idea of " 简 洁 " (concise and compact) implying an embrace of diversity while subtly forming things to fit ones needs.

Japan is an island country, 80% of which is covered by mountains and forests. To cope with the harsh living environment caused by sudden earthquakes, climatic disasters, the long wars during the Sengoku period, and poverty, people developed their skills and wisdom, which has been passed down and integrated into design aesthetics.

Contemporary Japanese design

The year 1990 witnessed a prosperous time of Japanese graphic design. Supported by the country's flourishing economy, graphic design was developing independently from international influences.

Along with the development of printing technology, Japanese arts gradually earned worldwide respect. We regard this process as Galapagosization. Posters designed by Makoto Saito, Seiju Toda, and Tsuguya Inoue exemplify their arduous efforts to present a strong visual impact by eliminating unnecessary details and redundant repetition. Many iconic pieces emerged from this novel aesthetic that had never been seen before. Japan is a nation-state with people speaking a uniform language. Thus the Japanese possess a tacit mutual understanding more felt, contextual, and visual than linguistic. Wordings like "Better keep it to yourself" and "Give the eye" were born in such a cultural circumstance. If co-creators do not need to elaborate to understand each other, then more tacitly intuited artistic expressions become possible, allowing unique fine arts designs to come into being. Awaiting Japan after the boom, however, was the breakdown of the bubble economy. Japanese graphic design, however unique, had actually been walking on eggs before plunging into a deep, dim abyss.

The 2003 Icograda Congress Nagoya's theme was Quality of Information: VISUALOG. Design projects were conducted around Kenya Hara, TakuSatoh, Osamu Fukushima, myself, and some others.

This event was to convey the idea that graphic design is not superficial creation; rather, it captures the essence of a message, to present the nature of things.

Japanese graphic design is about to show its talents. Those efforts spent in bewilderment are definitely not a waste of time. They constitute the preparation for a promising future. Japanese graphic design is no longer designs of Galapagosization, but fresh and clear creations arising from soft, tender presentations combined with local customs, regional features, and traditional ideology. It takes root deep into the soil of Japan. Finally, Japanese designers can proudly announce: "It comes from Japan."

> Graphic design in Japan tends to be simple, flat, and minimally stereoscopic, exuding a sense of cleanness and freshness. Through the works presented herein, do you share the aesthetic awareness infused deeply in Japan?

The Aesthetics of Flatness in Japanese Graphic Design

Eisuke Tachikawa

| Director

| NOSIGNER

Founding NOSIGNER while still a student, Eisuke Tachikawa is a design strategist who pursues a multi-disciplinary approach. Today, he serves as CEO of NOSIGNER and strives to produce social innovation through his activities. He has provided a wide range of innovative design encompassing science and technology, education, local industries, and more. His works have been acclaimed internationally, winning numerous global awards: the Design for Asia Grand Award, the iF Design Award, the Pentawards Platinum, the SDA Grand Award, and others. He was also appointed as the concept director for the Cool Japan Movement Promotion Council, by the Japanese government in 2014. Alongside his career as a designer, Eisuke is a passionate educator. He inspires students through his workshops on the Grammar of Design and his advice on design and innovation. He currently teaches at Keio University Graduate School of System Design and Management and Hosei University. He holds a Master's degree in Architecture from the Keio University Department of Science and Technology.

Modern Japanese graphic design was influenced by Typography from European in the 60s and gradually developed its own characteristics. Though still influenced by the West, it has cultivated a unique, inimitably soft aesthetic. From whence does this peculiar awareness arise? It is derived from the culture that existed before the word *design* was invented. To further explain these roots, I will briefly talk about the history of arts and culture in Japan.

Japan is an island nation neighboring China and has been influenced by Chinese culture since 2 B.C. Yet, the sea between Japan and China is the most dominant factor that contributed to the development of Japan's independent aesthetic awareness.

There was a time when it cost a great deal to cross the sea. In the case of the delegation sent from Japan to China during the Tang Dynasty, arranging for the ships was a huge difficulty. Great attention was paid to the ferry between the two countries.

Possible routes of embassy vessels to the Tang dynasty

Because of that, gifts from China were strictly selected. The treasures stored up in the Shosoin of Nara proves that, considering the high cost of transportation, gifts sent between the two countries had to meet the highest standards. This applied not only to goods manufactured in China, but also goods carried to Japan along the Silk Road.

In other words, the sea served as a filter to improve the quality of cultural communication. Despite the limited transmission of Chinese arts and crafts, Japan was fortunate enough to winnow out only the finest. Appreciating these beautiful things, Japan was admiring this remote country, trying to learn from Wang Xizhi and study calligraphy of Tang Dynasty. Japan merged Buddhism which was spread from China, with Shinto originating in the natural beliefs of ancient Japan and gradually reinterpreted it to cultivate its unique way.

Inspired by far-flung cultures, Japanese art, which long had been learning Chinese techniques, started to pursue its unique methods of expression. Based on the layered gradations of Chinese ink painting, Japanese painting began to pursue a flat style featured by the Rinpa school and Yamato-e. During the same period, merging with Buddhist beliefs, expressions found in, for example, Sado (Japanese tea ceremony), Ikebana (Japanese art of flower arrangement), and jewelry and accessories for Japanese feudal warlords were developed in a simple and highly abstract way. At that time, Japan created hiragana out of cursive script and started to use three kinds of typefaces: kanji, katakana, and hiragana. The impression of Japan the Beautiful originates from this period. During the Edo period, about 300 years ago, due to the isolationist policies, contact with the outside world was cut off, so the graphic aesthetic of flatness found in Yamato-e had its chance to spread through the grassroots, who were desperate for cultural commodities. In this way, inspired by Yamato-e and Komon (fine patterns), at last Japanese graphic design found its irreplaceable position in the world.

Japan's unique graphic aesthetics sprouted during the Age of Discovery, approximately 400 years ago. During the Momoyama period, Japan was enjoying an age of flourishing culture and was about to welcome the renaissance of Japanese culture.

Map of Japan in the Azuchi-Momoyama period.

Japanese embassy to the Tang court

Japanese painting depicting a group of Portuguese foreigners

If one really looks into modern Japanese graphic design, which offers an aesthetic awareness of flatness, you will find that it shares the same graphic style as other Japanese arts. There is a tendency toward minimal layers, clear composition, high abstraction, and chaste simplicity. In addition, a large number of independent typefaces were created to balance these complexly mixed types, and in particular, to express emotions and affections through design.

Thus, Japanese graphic design was developed through concepts of simple honesty, the beauty of compositional flatness, abstract shaping, and emotion-embodied typefaces. They are deeply rooted in Japanese graphic design. Will they be expanded to include more possibilities when deeply integrated into designs from other Asian countries? If this book can lead you into the essence of Japanese graphic design, I will be more than honored.

POSTWAR
FORTY YEARS

008 / 023

"I believe that visual communication is a common language of human beings and should be regarded in this way. "

"Therefore, Japanese graphic design needs first to reach the world standard. Only based on that can our graphic expression demonstrate the spirit of Japan. Traditions refer not only to traditional patterns or techniques, but more profoundly, it should be seen as an expression of spirituality."

Yusaku Kamekura (1915–1997)
— The father of Japanese Graphic Design

After the World War II, Kamekura emerged as an influential design leader who strived to develop Japan's design industry and earned his unshakable position as the father of Japanese graphic design.

Under his leadership, Japanese graphic designers abandoned the commonly held belief that visual communications must be hand-drawn. The notion of applied arts being inferior to fine arts was also weakened as Japanese designers gradually established their professional status.

POSTWAR 40 YEARS From 1950s to 1980s

During the postwar period, Japan experienced a rapid economic recovery, which enabled Japanese design to sparkle out its unique power.

Japan is an Eastern country with a profound history. Japanese design is largely different from Western design, both in cultural traditions and in ethnic aesthetics. Yet, to gain a reputation from the international market, Japan had to develop Internationalist, non-Japanese design style. Nonetheless, it never ceased protecting traditional and ethnic elements from the influence of economic activities and international trade competition.

Therefore, the audiences of Japanese graphic design can naturally be divided into two markets:

Designs aimed at the international market tend to present an international style with a corresponding design method to arouse widespread awareness.

Designs for the domestic market, however, are more likely to adhere to tradition, including traditional patterns, layouts and Chinese characters.

A History of Graphic Design, Chapter 16, by Wang Shouzhi

Constructivism:

It was an artistic and architectural philosophy originating in Russia. With a rejection to the idea of autonomous art, this movement claimed art can be "constructed" Its effect on modern art movements was pervasive, influencing major trends such as the Bauhaus and De Stijl movements.

Keywords: Western modern art, Constructivism

Since the 1950s, Japanese designers have started to comprehensively learn from modernist design by reviewing and interpreting it historically. Because Japanese rationality had a lot in common with European Constructivism, Japanese designers showed a special preference for this artistic idea.

The systematic organization and geometric construction of Constructivism really fascinated Japanese designers. Yet the Japanese more often apply central placement and organize space around a median axis, rather than employing the asymmetrical balance of European Constructivism.

Symmetric placement around a median axis is one of the components of traditional Japanese design.

Japanese design learned from European Constructivism and transformed it based on its own principles and preferences. Some symbolic elements were used in Japanese-style Constructivism, such as flowers, birds, animals, plants, and household objects.

2012, *SIZUYAPAN*, design: VATEAU

The rooted preference for vertical and horizontal lines and basic geometric shapes in traditional Japanese culture is the main reason why postwar Japanese design showed deep interest in Constructivism.

1934, *Composition*, design: Henryk Berlewi

First Generation

Yusaku KAMEKURA ———— Founder ————

Japan Advertising Artists Club (JAAC)

Established in 1951, the JAAC gradually became the core of Japan's design industry, raising Japan's graphic and industrial design to an international level. In 1970, due to cultural revolutions and student movements, it became a target of criticism and later dissolved in spite of its fame.

Keywords: international, ethnic

Kamekura's designs are always characterized by a conspicuously modern sense while often evoke the ethnic traditions of Japanese art. The visual system he created for the 1964 Tokyo Olympics is regarded as a paradigm of the combination of ethnicity and modernity.

Yoshio HAYAKAWA ———— Founder ————

Keywords: watercolor, feminine beauty

The use of materials, such as watercolor and toner, is Hayakawa's greatest strength. His posters were created in a lucent and soft manner to show a sense of romantic charm infused with ambiguous gloom and poetics, so much so that they seem to imply the feminine beauty of Japanese women.

Tadashi MASUDA ———— Founder ———— **MasudaTadashi Design Institute**

Keyword: photographic element

Masuda is one of the pioneers emerged during the postwar period. In his works, strong contrast of colors and forms was applied to strengthen the theme. He is the earliest advocate to apply a photographic approach to design.

Modern design development in Japan was well organized.

Personal and private organizations, together with government-sponsored activities, were great accelerators of graphic design development.

Kazumasa NAGAI

Keywords: linear form, traditional Japanese decoration

Nagai's oeuvre was constantly looking into linear form and the properties of line as a graphic medium for spatial modulation. His design approach, similar to system design, can always be traced to traditional Japanese folk decoration and design.

Ikko TANAKA

Keywords: planes, Japanese traditional motifs

Plane and form shape the core of Tanaka's works. Two underlying visual axioms in much of his works are grid structures and vibrant planes of color that explore warm-cool contrasts, close-valued color, and analogous color ranges. Traditional Japanese motifs, including landscape, Kanze Noh theater, calligraphy, masks, and woodblock prints, are reinvented in a modernist design idiom. In some of his most original works, color planes are arranged on a grid to signify abstracted and expressive portraits.

Igarashi TAKENOBU

Keyword: architectural alphabets

Takenobu is the first Japanese designer who designed a set of internationally recognized Western alphabet. He blended Eastern and Western ideas through his experiments with alphabets drawn on isometric grids. This isometric alphabets have evolved into three-dimensional alphabetic sculptures that Takenobu called *architectural alphabets*.

International Typographic Style:

The International Typographic Style, also known as the Swiss Style, is a graphic design style that emerged in Russia, the Netherlands and Germany in the 1920s, and was made famous as it was developed by designers in Switzerland during the 1950s. It emphasizes cleanliness, readability and objectivity. Hallmarks of the style are asymmetric layouts, use of a grid, sans-serif typefaces such as Akzidenz Grotesk, and flush-left, ragged-right text.

Third Generation

Shigeo FUKUDA

Keywords: figure-ground illusion, humor

Fukuda is regarded as one of the three greatest graphic designers in the world, along with Gunter Rambow and Seymour Chwast. His early experience of creating comics endowed him with a strong sense of humor. Yet, his designs are created to meet the international needs, without particular features of traditional Japanese paintings. He took good use of figure-ground illusion to create an optical illusion, making his works full of satire and playfulness.

Tadanori YOKOO

Keyword: Japanese Pop-up

Yokoo is the first Japanese designer who combined folk art with modern art and applied it to graphic design. From the mid-1960s, Yokoo started to use the comic-book technique of black-line drawing in his illustrations in which flat areas were applied with photomechanical color. He often collaged photographic elements into his designs, and translated traditional Japanese images into the Pop Art idiom. His works revealed restless vitality of Dada and Surrealism while taking reference from Japanese folk arts and Ukiyo-e themes, which shaped his distinctive Japanese Pop-up style.

Koichi SATO

Keyword: Zen Buddhism

Among the wave of the commercial design during the last century, Sato is one of the minority who strived to explore the cultural connotations of graphic design. His poster designs are characterized by the Zen Buddhism—calm, quiet, clean and modest. Sato thinks in opposites: traditional/futuristic, East/West, light/dark. His understanding of metaphysical poetics made him popular among Japanese culture atmosphere which flavors nonverbal communication and metaphorical language.

Kohei SUGIURA

Keyword: philosopher of design

Sugiura is a graphic designer, book designer, and design theorist with a solid academic background. He developed his own theory of perception, visual communication, and the essence of typography to make information vivid. Known as a pioneer scholar of Asian iconography and international infographic architect, Sugiura jettisoned mysterious Japanese elements in his designs, making him an outlier of Japanese design of his day.

Katsumi ASABA

Keyword: pictographic script

Asaba has a strong interest in Asian language, especially its pictographic scripts. He is a foundation member of the Tokyo Type Directors Club and a committee member of the ADC (Tokyo Art Directors Club). He transformed a surviving pictographic script, Dongba (Tompa), used by the Naxi tribe in China, into a personal design language titled Katsumi Asaba's Tompa Character Exhibition: The Last Living Pictographic Script on Earth. Nowadays, his study towards typeface has extended to areas such as Arabia, India, Thailand.

After 40 years of postwar recovery, modern graphic design in Japan has developed its own system.

The postwar miracle of Japan, which rose from the ashes of defeat to become a leader in technology and manufacturing, is paralleled by its emergence as a major center for graphic creativity. For 40 years, Japan kept absorbing nutrients from Western cultures and arts, but did not blindly imitate Western design style. Instead, they strived to combine the International Typographic Style with Japanese ethnic design. Up until the 1990s, modern Japanese design had received more and more worldwide recognition, which proved that Japanese approach to maintain and protect traditional culture is feasible.

Pop Art :

Pop Art, short for Popular Art, is also called New Realism. Pop Art emerged in the mid-1950s in Britain and the late 1950s in the United States. Pop Art, as Richard Hamilton, the father of Pop Art defined it in a now famous letter to the architects Alison and Peter Smithson, was: "Popular (designed for a mass audience), Transient (short-term solution), Expendable (easily forgotten), Low cost, Mass produced, Young (aimed at youth), Witty, Sexy, Gimmicky, Glamorous, and Big business."

Japanese graphics and Zen Buddhism :

Japanese graphics hardly use text explanation, sometimes even titles are eliminated, for text isn't the most important element for them. This mindset probably originates from Zen Buddhism 's intuitive understanding ("getting it").

Around 1953 to 1954, a wave of boycotting Japanese products took place in the world market, almost resulting in the stagnation of Japan's export trade. Japan demanded a reply from the UN concerning this matter, yet received only the feedback that Japan needed originality—designing products of its own characteristics. Thus, the Japanese government gathered a group of graduates from the Tokyo School of Fine Arts (later merged into Tokyo University of the Arts), and assigned them to different industries for design activities. In fact, Japan had established schools for arts and crafts since Meiji period, which laid a solid foundation of the rapid postwar development of design education.

At that time, Japan's universities had not founded specific departments of design, and their absorption of Western design relied on overseas students sponsored by the government. Since the 1950s, Japan's export trade organization would select five or six students each year and support their overseas design studies; it also held national high-end design seminars on a regular basis.

In 1975, the Tokyo University of the Arts set up a department of design, making it a department independent from crafts. This event has played a continuing and important role in the history of Japanese graphic design.

Ever since the status of design as an independent subject was recognized, together with indispensable support from the government, more and more comprehensive universities of Japan set up their own design departments, and some vocational design schools have gradually begun to make their name.

Top Graphic Design Institutions in Japan

Tokyo University of the Arts

Kyoto City University of Arts

University of Tsukuba

Joshibi University of Art and Design

Musashino Art University

Tama Art University

Kanazawa College of Art

Osaka University of Arts

Kyushu Institute of Design

Kobe Design University

Kuwasawa Design School

Japanese Design's Postwar Recovery Timeline

1950, The Tokyo Advertising Writer Club was founded.
In 1951, Ayao Yamana, Seiichiro Arai, Takashi Kono, Yusaku Kamekura, Hiromu Hara, Takeji Imaizumi and kinkichi Takahashi founded the Japan Advertising Artists Club.

1951, The Japan Advertising Artists Club was established.
During that time, exhibitions held by the Japan Advertising Artists Club and the Japan Industrial Designers' Association (JIDA) together became the most important platforms for young designers to present themselves.

1953, The Japan Advertising Federation was established; the World Poster Exhibition was held.

1954, The GLOBIS · Bauhaus Exhibition was opened in Tokyo.

1955, The Mainichi Industrial Design Award (renamed as Mainichi Design Awards) was set up; the Graphic '55 Exhibition was held.
The Mainichi Industrial Design Awards was set by Mainichi Shimbun, aiming to encourage designers help boost Japanese economy. Sori Yanagi, Chikara Watanabe, Isamu Kenmochi and more have received this awards. In 1976, it was renamed as the Mainichi Design Awards to include wider variety of design.

1957, The Good Design Products Selection System (G Mark system) is founded.
The Good Design Product Selection System as sponsored by the Ministry of International Trade and Industry was ended in 1997, and relaunched as the privatized Good Design Awards under the sponsorship of the Japan Industrial Design Promotion Association to find good designs and communicate them to society.

1959, The 21 Association was set up.
This association was formed by one of the first groups of young designers, such as Yusaku Kamekura, Hiromu Hara, Sugiura Kohei, Ikko Tanaka, Kazumasa Nagai, Mitsuo Katsui.

1960, The Nippon Design Center (NDC) was established and the World Design Conference was held in Tokyo.
Japan's top designers, copywriters, and photographers joined together as a creative organization aiming to further develop and improve the quality of advertising design in Japan.

1964, The 18th Olympics was held in Tokyo.
A series of visual designs for this Olympics has been highly praised, arousing Japanese' awareness of the importance of design in shaping Japan's image.

1969, The Japan Industrial Design Promotion Organization (JIDPO) was established.

During the journey of promoting Japanese graphic design, the government and educational institutions played significant roles respectively. Yet, industrial organizations led by designers acted as the most crucial and leading roles.

Art Director & Designer: Takeo Nakano
Programming: Masahiko Furukata
Gift Acknowledgement: Poster by Kazumasa
Nagai, Ikko Tanaka, Shigeo Fukuda, Eiko Ishioka
2015

Musashino Art University and Design V:

Japanese Graphic Design from the 1960s to the 1980s

Being the fifth entry in the Musashino Art University and Design series, which explores the history of modern design through works in the institution's collection, this exhibition focuses on graphic design in Japan during the period of rapid economic growth, from the 1960s to the 1980s. Visitors may explore that history through posters created since the day when improvements in printing technologies made greater stylistic diversity possible and the profession of designer became recognized.

Eiko Ishioka (1932-2012)

Born in Tokyo, Japan, Eiko Ishioka followed her ambition as a professional artist and designer after graduating from Tokyo National University of Fine Arts and Music. During her early career, she designed for advertising and printing. She later turned to theatre and movie costume design. In 1980s, Eiko Ishioka moved to New York. As she became more international, she started to review Japan from the perspective of an outsider. The Japanese traditional culture that once confined her provided her with a brand new dimension of thinking and helped create her unique style—a calm combination of the East and the West.

Throughout her entire career, Eiko Ishioka dealt with a wide range of design activities, including photography, music video, costume design, advertising, and graphic media. In 1985, she was chose to be the production designer for a 1985 film, *Mishima: A Life in Four Chapters*. Her excellent work went on to win her a special award for artistic contribution at the Cannes Film Festival that year. In 1987, Eiko won a Grammy Award for her artwork for Miles Davis' album *Tutu*. Eiko Ishioka made her way from being a graphic designer to one of the most eminent international Japanese art directors in several decades.

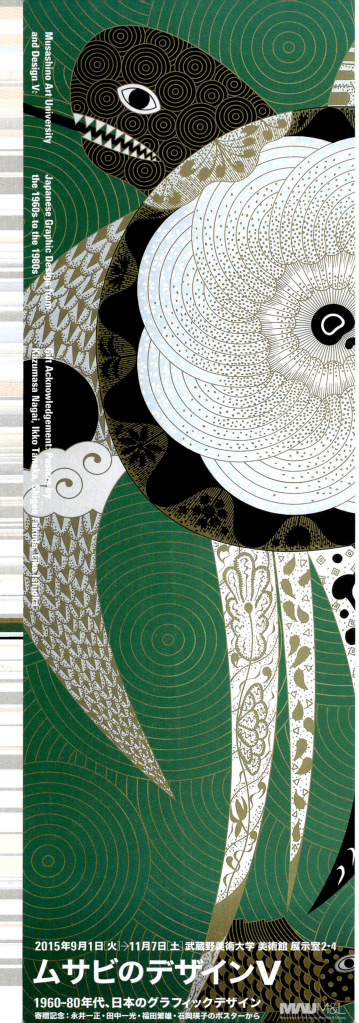

Musashino Art University and Design V:

Japanese Graphic Design from the 1960s to the 1980s

Gift Acknowledgement: Posters by Kazumasa Nagai, Ikko Tanaka, Shigeo Fukuda, Eiko Ishioka

2015年9月1日[火]→11月7日[土] 武蔵野美術大学 美術館 展示室2・4

ムサビのデザインV

018 1960-80年代、日本のグラフィックデザイン
寄贈記念：永井一正・田中一光・福田繁雄・石岡瑛子のポスターから

MAU M&L

2015年9月1日[火]→11月7日[土] 武蔵野美術大学 美術館 展示室2・4

ムサビのデザインV

1960-80年代、日本のグラフィックデザイン
寄贈記念：永井一正・田中一光・福田繁雄・石岡瑛子のポスターから

MAU M&L

Art Director & Designer: Takeo Nakano
Programming: Masahiko Furukata
Gift Acknowledgement: Poster by Kazumasa
Nagai, Ikko Tanaka, Shigeo Fukuda, Eiko Ishioka

2015

Kazumasa NAGAI

1988, Japan

1966, Growth – Life Science Library

Art Director & Designer: Takeo Nakano
Programming: Masahiko Furukata
Gift Acknowledgement: Poster by Kazumasa
Nagai, Ikko Tanaka, Shigeo Fukuda, Eiko Ishioka

2015

Ikko TANAKA

1981, Nihon Buyo Series

1961, Kanze Noh Play

Director & Designer: Takeo Nakano
Programming: Masahiko Furukata
Gift Acknowledgement: Poster by Kazumasa
Nagai, Ikko Tanaka, Shigeo Fukuda, Eiko Ishioka

2015

Shigeo **FUKUDA**

1945, Victory 1945

1984, Look 1

**GOLDEN
TEN YEARS**

024 / 043

As Japan's economy sped into the fast lane, it showed signs of becoming a counterpart of Europe and the U.S. Along Japan's path from imitation to original creation, this period is a crucial turning point:

From emphasizing the harmonious blend of the West and the East to concentrating on its own ethnic art and culture.

This transition laid the foundation of the specific style of Japanese graphic design.

2013,
151E,
design:
DEE LIGHTS

Ethnicity is obviously shown in Japanese-style packaging design. From texture, technologies, trademarks, patterns, to structure, all demonstrates Japanese cultural and artistic characteristics.

The Subject of Design

Graphic designers emerging in the late 80s and 90s are of the generation that experienced the ups and downs of the Japanese economy while witnessing the fierce collision between international artistic and cultural movements and ethnic and traditional cultures of Japan, along with the big picture of information technology development. Against this historical backdrop, Japanese designers not only generated a rebellious spirit, but relentlessly explored the purpose of graphic design. These attempts centered around two issues: (a) design and humanity and (b) design and life, which concluded that the subject of design is humanity.

GOLDEN 10 YEARS
1990s

Keywords: post-modernism, digital technologies

With post-modernism exercising more influence on Japan's national thought, Japanese graphic designers started to find their way away from the so-called authorities and classics, exploring graphic design within an alternate era of old and new values.

Meanwhile, digital technologies enabled graphic design to imagine a larger and more daring concept of creativity. Especially when Macintosh became popular through its low price, many ideas that had been unachievable before came into being, creating an energetic and diverse graphic design industry.

During the mid- and late 80s, Japanese design paid far more attention to appearance than function, which, to some extent, reflected the bubble economy of the time.

Keyword: ideology of graphic design

During the early 90s, Japan's economic bubbles completely burst, causing a series of social problems. Japanese graphic designers started to think about design's social responsibilities and respond to these social issues, in the hope of influencing citizens' mindsets and making positive explorations of economic recovery.

During this period, Japanese designers attached great attention to the subject of design.

How to design → **How to communicate**

The focus of design transformed from design techniques to humanistic spirit.

Makoto SAITO

Keyword: loose boundry of design and art

Poster master.

In Saito's designs, he actively changed the way how humans and their cultural environment react with each other. Almost entirely devoid of text, Saito's designs apply elements of the human body to transmit the spirit of art by means of black-and-white contrast, figure-ground illusion, and photographic collage. These artistic techniques of expression blur the boundaries between commercial purpose and artistic pursuit. The creation of his works went from static to dynamic, making the visual space more open and intensive.

Kaoru KASAI

Keyword: humanistic thinking

The recorder of times.

Kasai's works are always full of humanistic thinking and convey a sense of tranquility. His early experience in layout and typeface design made him meticulous about details. Throughout the ten golden years of Japanese advertisement, Kaoru Kasai kept exploring as many design fields as possible, including movies, books, space, and corporate identity.

Graphic design of post-modernism:

Originating from architecture in the late 1970s, post-modernism embodies some obvious features of architectural drawings, such as meaningful combinations of geometric shapes and three-dimensional typeface, which are nowhere to be found in the International Typographic Style.

Although post-modernism can be traced back to modernism, it has been focused on the decorative dimension of design. It broke down the dullness of rationality by using decorative patterns, bold and vivid colors, and various typefaces, conveying a strong visual impact on the audience.

During the 1980s, economies of the U.S., Europe, and Japan were developing at an astonishing speed, which gave birth to a new generation of consumers—the Me Generation—who were an important accelerator for post-modernism becoming popular in graphic design. Magnificent colors, delicate decorative elements, and strong personal expression all meet up in designs of the time, which also reflected the overall impression of graphic design in Japan during bubble economy -positive, humorous, self-centered.

Seiju TODA

Keyword: catch the ephemeral

Toda has been interested in the ephemeral since the mid-1960s, when he began his artistic career. Since the mid-1970s, he has been using various media to play with issues that preoccupy contemporary artists, such as the human eye's imperfect recognition of reality, different experience of reproductive media, the process of art making, the very nature of art, the representation of motion and light. Toda used simple yet fundamental materials, such as wood, water, light, and living creatures to make arts, which goes in line with Japanese art, complimented by subdued colors, strict geometries, careful symmetry, and a studied tranquility.

Shin MATSUNAGA

Keyword: creation comes from daily iterms

The experience of material deprivation during Matsunaga's early life made him acknowledge the invaluable happiness that nature provides to a person and helped develop his love for a simply yet satisfied lifestyle. He designed with the approach of picking up overlooked daily objects, eliminating the unnecessary and presenting only the nature. In this way, the beauty and information intended were magnified. His creative world has been described as the "three-meter radius" philosophy, meaning that he gains inspiration from objects within three meters of wherever he is.

Kenya HARA

Keyword: haptic, re-design, emptiness

Being one of the pillar designers in Japan, Hara bases his design beliefs on daily life and re-designs familiar things into something unfamiliar. His product designs does not go out of its way to influence and shape customers but rather invites the them to fill in the "void" for their own self-expression and utility. He combines tactile senses and Japanese Zen Buddhism with his designs, creating a unique sense of emptiness.

Japanese Aesthetic Basics
Part One

わび - さび
Wabi – Sabi

IDEALISTIC AESTHETICS

Keywords: Zen Buddhism, poetic tendency

Influenced deeply by Chinese Taoism and Zen Buddhism, Wabi-Sabi's philosophy, spirit, and moral principles can be traced back to people thinking about nature and the universe; its empty and lonely space as well as minimalistic forms come from Chinese poems and ink wash paintings.

Wabi-sabi is originally an obscure expression. During the 14th century, however, some hermits and ascetics lived in desolation and solitude, exploring Zen philosophy and spiritual world. Gradually, this way of living became well recognized and even regarded as a means to enrich one's spiritual life and improve one's appreciation of daily details and simple objects. This poetic tendency transformed the negative meaning of wabi-sabi to a positive one.

Wabi-Sabi and Modernism

Similarity

- both are a reversible force of the mainstream of the time;

- abstract beauty of non-representation;

- recognizable characteristics—modernism favors flawless design while wabi-sabi prefers plain and imperfect.

Difference

Wabi-Sabi	intuitional	warm	perceptive	more haptic & vague	blurred lines & shapes
Modernism	reasoning & logic	cold	functional	less haptic & definite	accurate & clear straight geometric lines

HE KNOWS MOST WHO SPEAKS LEAST

Wabi-Sabi is an aesthetic concept indescribable through reasoning.

The Japanese have always avoided giving clear definitions of wabi-sabi, partly because this aesthetic was developed from Zen. As is commonly known, rather than explicitly explain meaning through words, Zen prefers intuitive understanding, or just "getting it". On the other hand, the iemoto system is entangled in Japanese corporate culture, combined with wabi-sabi's philosophy, making it an excellent marketing strategy. Therefore, wabi-sabi cannot be described in detail. Besides, even though this aesthetic concept is deeply rooted in the bones and blood of the Japanese, there are no books dedicated to defining what it is.

Iemoto System:

Iemoto is a Japanese term referring to the founder or current Grand Master of a certain school of traditional Japanese art, such as tea ceremony, ikebana, calligraphy, or martial arts. The iemoto system is characterized by a hierarchical structure and the supreme authority of the iemoto, who has inherited the secret traditions of the school from the previous iemoto.

He served as one of Toyotomi Hideyoshi's three tea masters, along with Tsuda Sogyu and Imai Sokyu, and is now known as the Japanese tea saint.

Sen no Rikyu (1522-1591)

Being popularized, developed and incorporated into the tea ceremony by Rikyu, the wabi-sabi aesthetic extended from the Japanese tea ceremony into other Japanese traditional arts–ikebana, the Japanese art of incense appreciation, Japanese poetry and so forth.

Until now, wabi-sabi has been immersed into everyday details of Japanese lives, and Japanese commercial society.

GET RID OF
ALL THAT IS
UNNECESSARY

**Pare down to the essence, but don't
remove the poetry;
keep things clean and unencumbered,
but don't sterilize.**

— Leonard Koren, *Wabi-Sabi: for Artists, Designers, Poets & Philosophers*

2012,
Musashino Art University,
design: Takao Minamidate

A series of posters created for the Musashino Art University by Takao Minamidate serves as an example. The main idea is to present the beauty of color. Edges of elliptical shapes show a gradual change of colors, conveying a clean and quiet sense of beauty.

Keyword: Japanese minimalism

Both being called "beautiful design" and regarded as minimalistic, Japanese design and Western design can be confusing sometimes. Yet, by knowing their respective origins and beliefs, it is much easier to distinguish them. It is just like the different feelings people experience when entering Muji and Ikea. These differences between them are shown in graphic design.

Compared with communicating certain messages visually to audiences, Japanese graphic design, which is based on wabi-sabi, emphasizes using associative images to guide the audiences to understand the intended meaning.

	Japan	**The West**
Origin	Zen Buddhism; material deprivation	Developed modern industry
Impression	Emptiness	Simplicity
Image	Leaving extensive blanks	Creating visual impacts by vivid and bold colors
Tendency	Constraint (This will do)	Open (This is what I really want)
Color	Plain, neat and quiet	Clear and sharp

"Because of the overload of information, we have been undergoing a state of uncertainty. Knowledge no longer acts as a medium to provoke our thinking. The accumulated information is like seeds that don't have a chance to sprout; it is degraded to an ambiguous situation, without knowing whether it is dead or alive."
— By Kenya Hara, *Design in Design*

To fight against the overload of information fraction is probably one of the reasons why wabi-sabi has become the mainstream idea of design in Japanese graphics.

INFORMATION → EXFORMATION

Exformation:

This is a term coined by a Danish author Tor Nørretranders in his book *The User Illusion: Cutting Consciousness Down to Size.* "Exformation", as he defined it, "is what is rejected en route, before expression." Kenya Hara writes in his book *Design in Design* that in an era of media evolving nonstop, every incident is processed as a certain kind of message and circulated in high intensity and velocity. By constantly receiving and sending information, the world changes from being the unknown to the known. However, what keeps us moving is the unknown. The known does not inspire us, yet we are eager to turn the world into the known.

**Muji, shortened for Mujirushi Ryohin,
translates as "no-brand quality goods."**

It began as a product brand of the supermarket chain, Seiyu, Ltd., in December of 1980. In the early 1980s, mainstream Japanese graphic design employed strong visuals to enforce brand recognition, applying effective decoration to distinguish one brand from others. At that time, Seiji Tsutsumi, President of the Seiyu, Ltd., believed that the whole market was overwhelmed with colors, so he initiated the concept of anti-brand. To begin with, he gathered a few famous designer friends, including Ikko Tanaka, Kazuko Koike, Masaru Amono, Takashi Sugimoto, and thoroughly discussed this concept, eventually opening Muji under the auspices of Seiyu, Ltd. In 2002, after Ikko Tanaka passed away, Kenya Hara, one of the pillars of Japanese design, took over the art director position.

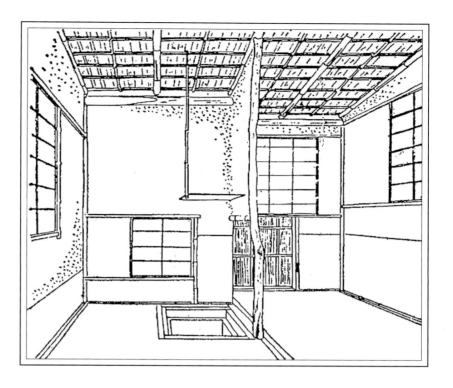

THE TALE OF JAPANESE TEA CEREMONY
The two-tatami mat tea room of Sen no Rikyu

Tea Monk:
A position that Buddhist monks take to serve tea. The term dates back to the Chixiu Baizhang Qinggui (The Imperial Edition of Baizhang's Rules of Purity), composed by Dongyang Dehui in 1338.

Tatami:
A type of mat used as a flooring material in washitsu (traditional Japanese-style rooms). Often room size can be measured in terms of tatami. Tea rooms are usually four and a half tatami, that is, 6.97 square meters. Two tatami mats are equal to 3.24 square meters.

After the death of his master, Joo Takeno, Sen no Rikyu further developed his preceptor's heritage technique of chanoyu, the Japanese Way of Tea, to an unprecedented level and became a tea master himself. Then, in 1579, Rikyu became a tea monk for Toyotomi Hideyoshi, to help at tea gatherings. His relationship with Hideyoshi quickly deepened, and he not only gave guidance in chanoyu, but also discussed political issues as a head of commerce. Hideyoshi was a natural in politics yet had a strong preference for luxury and extravagance. Under his orders, Rikyu designed the magnificent Golden Tea Room. However, the true tea room Rikyu had in mind was tiny, rustic, even shabby. He reformed the original space, of six-tatami mats, into four, then finally two, in keeping with Zen restraint.

The tea room door was small and low, like a dog door. In this way, one must bow down and lower one's head, crawling ahead. Samurai had to take off their sabers and leave them outside. Officers removed their hats because Rikyu taught that within the tea room all must leave behind all worldly status. The dim light and space, just large enough for doing nothing but sitting still, invited calm: the atmosphere of chanoyu.

PAINTING

Traditional Paintings
&
Modern Manga

In modern times, Japanese graphic design has constantly absorbed Western influences, combining them with traditional Japanese cultural elements to form a style both international and uniquely Japanese. More than any other traditional cultural element, Japanese painting penetrated national boundaries. In the West, where design and art had long dominated, Japanese painting flourished because part of the Art Nouveau movement during the transition from the 19th to the 20th century.

Japonaiserie:

Dutch post-impressionist painter Vincent van Gogh was perhaps the one most influenced by Ukiyo-e: so much so that he coined the term Japonaiserie to describe the influence of Japanese art. He parroted a large number of Ukiyo-e paintings and later integrated artistic factors of Ukiyo-e into his own works. His most renowned painting, *The Starry Night*, characterized by swirls, alludes to Hokusai Katsushika's *The Great Wave off Kanagawa*.

According to historical texts, Japanese paintings created for ornamental purposes derive from Chinese Tang Dynasty art: Kara-e is a name given to describe this particular style of Japanese painting. The style does not show any apparent sign of ethnicity.

In 894 B.C. (the Heian period), Japan abolished embassies to Tang Dynasty courts, and Japanese missions to Imperial China were stopped. From then on, Japan was no longer just adopting Tang models of social system, production, arts, and architecture: Japan was breaking the chains of Tang cultural influence. Yamato-e was born.

Moving forward to the 18th century (the Edo period), under the rule of the Tokugawa shogunate the national political situation was stable and its economy was improving. Urban commerce was developing diversely as citizens participated in more and more colorful activities.

To depict this social phenomenon, Ukiyo-e was born. Also, because of the use of full-color woodblock printing and the low cost of reproduction, Ukiyo-e effloresced in the late 17th century.

1832, *The Great Wave off Kanagawa*, by Hokusai Katsushika

1980, *The Starry Night*, by Vincent van Gogh
Current location: Museum of Modern Art (MoMA)

2014, *Ninigi*, design: Estudio Yeyé
This wall mural integrated the style of Yamato-e into its creation.

2012, *MICCHAN*, design: IC4DESIGN
This branding project made its reference to Ukiyo-e, combining techniques of modern illustration.

Kano School:

The Kano school is a Japanese painting doctrine that came into being among professional artists. They worked mainly for the nobility, dominating Japanese painting for around 400 years. Although this style made tribute to Chinese traditions in its theme and techniques, its expression were entirely Japanese. Its main characteristic is the bold and vigorous touch achieved by sharp, firm lines and light-and-dark contrast.

Rinpa School:

Established by Koetsu Honami and Sotatsu Tawaraya, the Rinpa school became fully accomplished through the efforts of Korin Ogata and Kenzan Ogata and officially recognized in Edo by Hoitsu Sakai and Kiitsu Suzuki.

Following the Yamato-e style, the Rinpa school pursued pure Japanese charm by using precious substances such as gold and silver. Bold layouts and striking color schemes, repeating patterns and advanced dripping techniques, are its most notable features. Classic Rinpa style involves simple, natural subjects such as birds and plants in the form of figure, Shan shui, and Buddhist paintings.

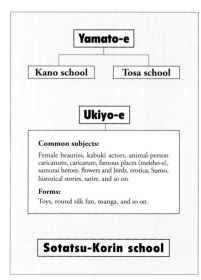

Yamato-e
— Kano school
— Tosa school

Ukiyo-e

Common subjects:
Female beauties, kabuki actors, animal-person caricatures, caricature, famous places (meisho-e), samurai heroes, flowers and birds, erotica, Sumo, historical stories, satire, and so on.

Forms:
Toys, round silk fan, manga, and so on.

Sotatsu-Korin school

(6)

(5)

(7)

1. Ban Dainagon Ekotoba (*The Tale of Great Minister Ban*) by Mitsunaga Tokiwa: a collection of Idemitsu Museum of Arts.

2. Choju-jinbutsu-giga (*Scrolls of Frolicking Animals*) by Sojo Toba: the first and third scrolls are in the collection of the Tokyo National Museum, whereas the second and fourth are in the Kyoto National Museum.

3&4. Shigisan-engi (*Legend of Mount Shigi*) resides in the collection of Chogosonshi-ji in Ikoma, Nara Prefecture, Japan.

5&6.Genji Monogatari Emaki (*The Tale of Genji*) resides separately in the Tokugawa Art Museum and Gotoh Museum.

7. *Birds and Flowers of the Four Seasons*, by Motonobu Kano, resides in the Hakutsuru Fine Art Museum.

8. *Waves at Matsushima*, by Sotatsu Tawaraya, is housed in The Smithsonian's Museum of Asian Art.

(8)

(1)

(2)

This is a style of Japanese painting coming from, yet fully distinguishable from Tang dynasty paintings. Developed from the late Heian period and all the way until the 19th century, Yamato-e often depicts Japanese culture and customs with a simplified and stylized . It is characterized as being secular and decorative, with a tradition of strong colors: human subjects are depicted with simple touches that yet retain the charm of their posture and facial expressions; the overall compositions are vigorous and flowing, showing traces of graphic design.

(3)

(4)

1. *South Wind, Clear Sky* (aka *Red Fuji*), one of the *Thirty-six Views of Mount Fuji* series, by Katsushika Hokusai.

2. *Benkei with Yoshitsune*, by Yoshitoshi Tsukioka.

3. *Beauty Looking Back*, by Moronobu Hishikawa.

4. *Couple Under Umbrella in Snow*, by Harunobu Suzuki.

5. *Three Beauties of the Present Day*, by Ichitaro Kitagawa.

6. *Nihon-ryakushi Susanoo-no-mikoto*, by Yoshitoshi Tsukioka.

7. *Kanbara* (*A village in the snow*), one of the *Fifty-three Stations of the Tokaido*, by Hiroshige Utagawa.

8. *Bake-Bake Gakko* (*School for Spooks*), by Kyosai Kawanabe.

9. *Elegant: A Lady of the Imperial Court in the Kyowa Period*, one of the *Thirty-two Aspects of Customs and Manners* series, by Yoshitoshi Tsukioka.

10. *Otani Oniji III in the Role of the Servant Edobei*, by Sharaku Toshusai.

(1)

(2)

Ukiyo, meaning floating world, refers to life during Japan's Edo period. Thus, ukiyo-e are paintings depicting anything reflecting that era. Ukiyo-e are always strongly decorative, because they were usually applied to wall murals of magnificent buildings or to folding screens decorating interiors. This style tends to choose scenes of the four seasons and famous places as its content, making it abound with local characteristics. Besides, it is especially good at presenting female beauties in realistic strokes. It includes a wide range of topics, from social issues, folk legends, and historical stories, to female lives, wars, and landscapes. Transcending the merely illustrative, it offers an encyclopedia of people's lives during Edo period.

(5)

(4)

(3)

MANGA (Japanese comics)

can date back to as early as Toba Sojo's animal scroll paintings (aka Choju Giga) in the 12th century. Manga of the Meiji period shares an intertwined history with the development of newspapers and periodicals in the late 19th century Japan. After the outbreak of World War II, manga were unpopular for a long time. During the postwar period, *Nakayoshi*, *Weekly Shonen Sunday*, *Weekly Shonen Magazine*, and *Weekly Shonen Jump* were established and published in succession, which means manga was reviving. Crucial figures, such as Osamu Tezuka, Shotaro Ishinomori, Fujio Akatsuka, and Fujio Fujiko emerged to play their roles in the development of manga. Shigeo Fukuda, one of the three most important graphic designers in the world, used to work in the manga industry, and this experience explicitly influenced him.

800 Years of Manga

Since the animal scroll paintings of the Heian period, the history of manga has survived more than 800 years. From the hand-paintings of ancient times, to woodblock painting and digital printing, the essence of manga—comical, humorous, sarcastic and fantastic—remains regardless of its creation technologies, styles, and era.

Japanese Oldest Manga—Choju Giga

A rabbit and frogs pursue a monkey thief (first scroll).

Animals taking baths (first scroll).

Men defeat each other in wrestling matches (fourth scroll).

The predecessor of Japanese Modern Manga—Hokusai Manga

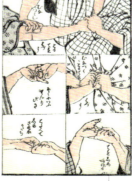

In Houkusai Manga, one can see the page composition change from dividing a whole page into two, three, and even four panels, which helped establish the form of modern four-panel comics.

Choju-jinbutsu-giga (*Scrolls of Frolicking Animals*):
As an ancient cultural property collected in the Kozan-ji temple (Kyoto), it is a set of four-picture scrolls that made fun of Japanese priests of the artist's time, characterizing them as toads, rabbits, and monkeys. The animals were drawn with expressive faces ("speed lines"), a technique used in manga till this day, Choju-jinbutsu-giga is credited as being the oldest work of manga in Japan.

Hokusai Manga:
The *Hokusai Manga* is a collection of sketches by the Japanese artist Katsushika Hokusai. The manga comprises of about 4 thousands images in 15 volumes, block-printed in three colors (black, gray and pale flesh). Its subjects include landscapes, flora and fauna, everyday life and the supernatural. It was first published in 1814 and was later used as a paradigm for painting learners. receiving high reputation even at that time.

The real industrialization of manga took place during the 1950s. Manga gradually became the main product of the entire publishing industry. As it evolved over time, due to its various topics and genres and successful managing system, its popularity has spread across the globe. The truth is when talking about manga, you will not skip mentioning Japan.

In commercial graphic design, works created in the form of manga will be loved by audiences because of their funny and amicable visuals.

2011, *Manga Plates*, design: Mika Tsutai
Combining the style and techniques of manga into the design of plates, the designer fully conveys the spirit of design and food placed altogether, transforming our dinner table into a story, just like reading pages of a Japanese comic.

2013, *World Table Tennis Championships*, design: Yuri Uenishi
This manga depicts a series of stories happening in a ping pong club of junior high school. The images of characters being mischievous in every way, such as showing the nostrils and gingiva, farting without shame, humorously present the combination of endless energy and sportsmanship.

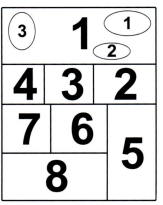

The proper order of reading modern manga
Manga consists of panels, gutters (space outside the panels), figures, backgrounds, dialog balloons and sound effects. Most manga is read from right to left. The same applies to dialog bubbles, words and sound effects. The image to the left shows the proper order and direction to read manga. Notably, this reading order is the same as that of traditional Japanese text.

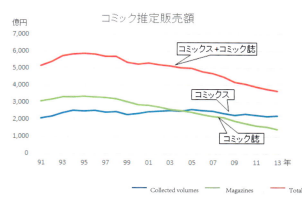

コミック推定販売額
億円

コミックス+コミック誌
コミックス
コミック誌

Collected volumes   Magazines   Total

Source: *Annual Report of the Publication Market 2014*, by The Research Institute for Publications (http://www.ajpea.or.jp/)

All around the world, compared with popular culture such as pop music, manga is usually regarded as a product of a subculture.

In the 1990s, manga reached the height of its dominance, by seizing half of the market share in publishing. Although the volume of distribution in recent years has shown signs of decreasing, as the table depicts, the number of those reading manga is still large and consistent. Above all, manga have been the main books Japanese children read for entertainment.

Manga magazines have been the main medium for Japanese comics. There are about 40 magazines that are comparatively influential: 13 of which are weekly published weekly, 10 bi-weekly, and about 20 monthly. Concerning the amount of distribution of each issue, the 14 most popular manga magazines have sold more than 1 million copies.

Subculture:
Derived from mainstream culture, subcultures normally are emerging cultures that are popular among minority of society. Whether an emerging culture can be included as popular culture is up to the media who have the platforms and channels to expose whatever they choose. Yet, not all manga have the chance to be promoted, let alone be regarded as part of the mainstream. For example, animated television programs launched in the 1970s were seen as children's entertainment. The notion was so deeply rooted that anime was an object of prejudice, to some extent. During the mid and late 1970s, this attitude changed slowly, with the popularity of anime being aimed at wider audiences, such as *Space Battleship Yamato*, *Lupin III*, and *Mobile Suit Gundam*.

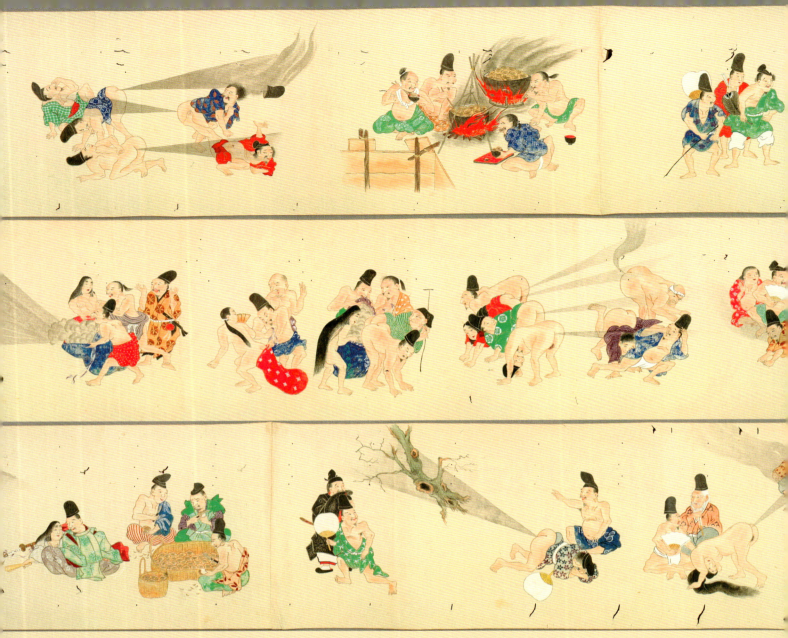

Hegassen Emaki (*Fart Battle*), medium: ink on paper, dimensions: 29.6cm×1003.1cm (11.7″×394.9″), current location: Waseda University Library. Find it online in http://wine.wul.waseda.ac.jp/, with call number チ 04 01029.

He-gassen is a series of Japanese art scroll created during the Edo period, literally meaning fart battle. It is said that the earliest person to explore this topic was Sojo Toba. Others, however, argued it was the artist-monk Jochi. Toba depicted fart battles in his work Katsu-e: one of the most well-known He-gassen scrolls, in the collection of the Waseda University Library. It was created during the Edo period by an unknown artist or several unknown artists. According to the inscription written at the end of the scroll—meaning "69 artists from Fukuyama city participated in the production and revision"—this scroll received more content, in 1846, by referencing ancient paintings created in 1680, by Hishikawa Moronobu. The funny part is, throughout the scroll, various scenes depict at least one character directing a cloud of flatulence toward other characters.

The Daily Mail reviewed this scroll, saying it "is in fact a pointed comment on political and social changes in Japan." Moreover, some argued this scroll and similar drawings were created in response to the suspicion of Tokugawa shogunate towards the increasing intrusion of Europeans and the ruthless persecution of Christians.

THE
21st CENTURY

The Mission and Responsibility of Design

I am aware that my perception of design has changed little by little in recent years ... ...

Eriko Kawakami

A member of JAGDA (Japan Graphic Designers Association). Awards include JAGDA Award in 2013, ADC Award in 2015 and JAGDA New Designer Award in 2016.

Packaging

Projects 046 / 105

Minimalism: Minimum Expression, Maximum Impression

I believe design has been endowed with the ability to convey the meaning that words fail to convey ... ...

Daigo Daikoku

Art Director of Daikoku Design Institute. Recipient of the JAGDA New Designer Award, the Tokyo ADC Prize and the D&AD Yellow Pencil Awards.

Branding

Projects 106 / 147

A Brief Talk About Japanese Aesthetics

I think the minimalism in graphic expression varies with the level of cultural maturity of a country ... ...

Ren Takaya

Graduated from Tohoku University of Art & Design in 1999. Recipient of the Cannes Lions, D&AD, NYADC, NYTDC, Hiiibrand Typography, JAGDA New Designer Award, Grand Prix, Gold Golden Bee 11.

Poster & Book

Projects 148 / 189

What's the Nature of Japanese Graphic Design ?

When we look back on history, it is said that Rinpa school, which was ... ...

Masaomi Fujita

Graduated from the Faculty of Design of Shizuoka University of Art and Culture. Established a design office tegusu in 2012.

Logo

Projects 190 / 221

Packaging

The Mission and Responsibility of Design

Eriko Kawakami
| Art Director
| Draft co., ltd.

Eriko Kawakami was born in 1982, in Tokyo, Japan. She graduated in 2006 from the Department of Design, Tokyo University of the Arts, and worked in Draft co., ltd. since 2008. Her main works include the branding of san grams, graphic designs for Pocchiri and the Aoyama Flower Market, and Art Director of NHK Heart Exhibition, designs for the product brand D-BROS, a branch of Draft co., ltd., and others. In addition, she is a member of JAGDA (the Japan Graphic Designers Association). Awards include the JAGDA Award, in 2013; the ADC Award, in 2015; and the JAGDA New Designer Award, in 2016.

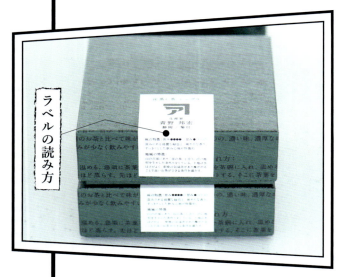

I am aware that my perception of design has changed little by little in recent years. I took part in a branding project, and it got me thinking about the mission, power, and responsibility of design.

It was three years ago when a century-old tea company in Shizuoka Prefecture called. We discussed that due to the massive use of PET bottles, sales of tea leaves that need a small teapot to brew were decreasing. Thus, they were striving to increase the value of tea and revitalize tea industry.

When I visited their company to garner more details, learned that because of the rapidly popularized PET bottle, tea companies have to produce large amounts of tea leaves of stable flavor to meet consumer's needs. Many peasant families merged together to form cooperatives. Therefore, independent peasant families producing tea leaves have become more and more rare. In fact, tea leaves in the market are mixed tea leaves provided by these cooperatives.

It is not necessarily a bad idea to mix tea leaves. One of the advantages these mixed tea leaves have is that leaves from different peasant families can produce a complementary and stable flavor. On the other hand, this uniform flavor cannot truly communicate the full an lingering charm of tea leaves.

So, we offered our solution: rather than focus on stable flavor and productivity, great attention should be paid to present the character of tea leaves that individual peasant families produce, to feature the unique charm of different tea varieties. Our idea came from wine tasting. As we all know, red wine is featured by different vintage years. When noticing the taste of red wine of different vintages, you genuinely begin to understand the charm of red wine.

I was informed that tea leaves that do not mix well with those of other peasant families are called single tea leaves. And I know single malt whiskey is a kind of whiskey made from a single distillery. I was inspired and wanted to make a name for single tea leaves, just like single malt whiskey, in order to make customers experience their unique features.

In addition, we opened a tea shop called san grams, which also served coffee. Japanese green teas, including Fukamushicha (deep steamed green tea), Kukicha (twig tea), Kabusecha (literally translated as covered tea), Houjicha (roasted tea), Oolong tea, and so forth, are best brewed with exactly three grams of tea leaves. The word three is pronounced san in Japanese. Through this name, we strived to communicate that to truly taste tea one should brew tea using the right process. As for the packaging, labels are attached, showing the trade name, producer, producing area, flavor, and characteristics. We also designed a slogan, meaning "We wish you an enjoyable taste of tea" and a leaflet that introduces the right way to brew tea. Once a month, we deliver lectures about brewing tea according to the history and the category of tea. For the tea shop's promotion, we designed a beverage- serving program to make coffee a supplementary part of tea tasting. To ensure that customers can cozily taste tea in the shop, we replaced half of the lawn with a courtyard of plants that change seasonally. In this way, from product packaging, catering, and interior space to the courtyard, the tea shop fully conveys the beauty and charm of tea.

Naturally, the marketing strategy was muted. In order to showcase the company's idea, the logo design is derived from the product's name, and references a traditional Japanese design. The main color of the packaging is determined the dark green of Fukamushicha, a specialty in Kikugawa, Shizuoka Prefecture, Japan. In addition, the tea brewing method appears on the surface of the tea box. The packaging of a confection is presented in a color that matches up with the tea color.

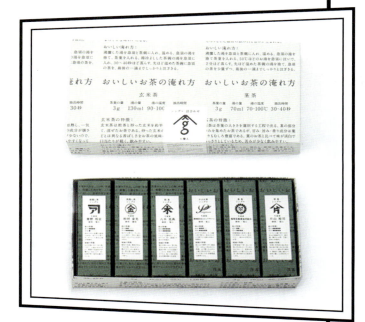

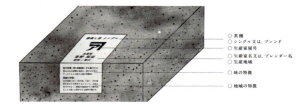

Why should I elaborate on this project in detail? Because before this project, I had been consciously pursuing modeling in design. For example, I would try to design the visual identity of this project by simply focusing aesthetic feeling and novelty. This certainly is part of the job of design, and when presenting aesthetic visuals, simplicity matters. Yet, if a design communicates a clear message but in a non-aesthetic way, it will hardly impress anyone. Thus, the message and the way of communicating the message are both important. To capture the true value of a product and to present it precisely through visual arts are two responsibilities that every designer should assume.

Through this project, I understand once again that it is of great significance to delve deeply into the features and value of a product, considering thoroughly how it can interact with the world before modeling. If this procedure goes well, effective modeling will naturally follow.

To present the natural beauty of Kyushu, the third largest island of Japan, this product packaging makes use of paper wrappings with a small piece of parallel strips of different colors resembling diverse bird feather colors.

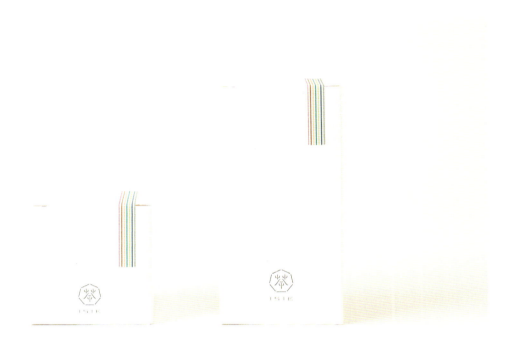

Studio: DEE LIGHTS

Kadokuwa

Kanroni, sweet dew shimmered fish, has been the most popular product of Kadokuwa since it was founded. To show this traditional Japanese cuisine method, the package was designed to visually reproduce the image of the tasteful and thick sauce.

あまごの甘露煮
佃煮の老舗 角繁商店

手持ち鮎の甘露煮
佃煮の老舗 角繁商店

鮎の甘露煮
佃煮の老舗 角繁商店

角繁商店
江戸末期創業 佃煮の老舗

Zen Kashoin

Zen Kashoin is a Japanese traditional sweets brand embodying the concept of "returning flowers and confectionery to their authentic state". The packages are full of Japanese design elements such the ruled lines of old textbooks and Japanese traditional plants drawn in sumi ink.

Party Popper

The designers built upon the features of ordinary party poppers, replacing the normal confetti with small, naturally falling forms rendered in paper: raindrops, cherry blossoms, falling leaves, snow.

さくら　　　あめ　　　おちば　　　ゆき

あめ

さくら

おちば

ゆき

Designers: Shogo Kishino & Miho Sakaki Studio: 6D

Harmonian

To convey an aura of harmony and balance, the designer created simple white packages which are distinguished by the illusion of a cut, a twofold spindle-like incision on paper.

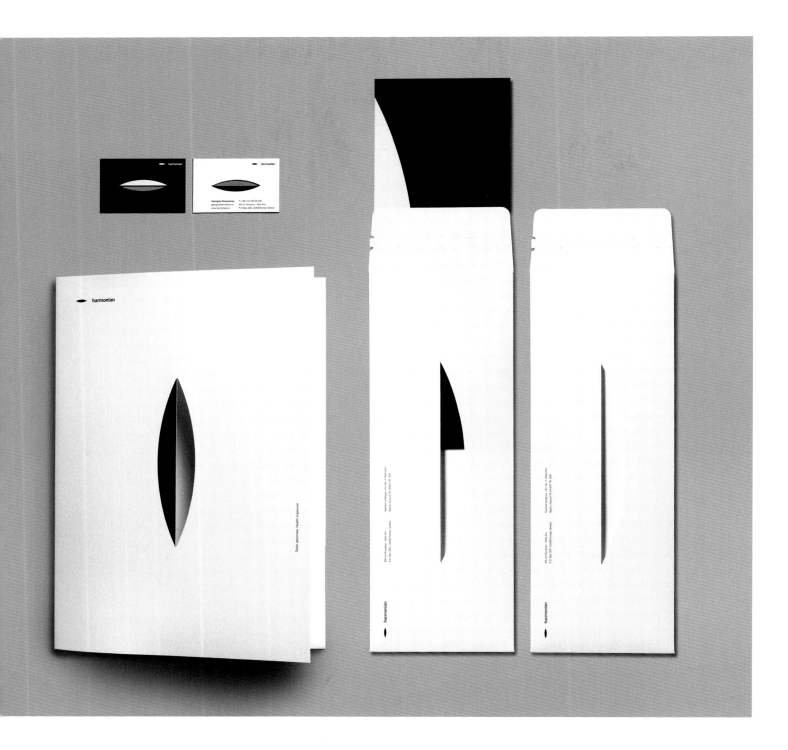

Designer: Joshua Olsthoorn   Studio: mousegraphics

Soutatu

This branding of sea tangle tried to convey the idea that sea tangle is not only a traditional ingredient, but also a contemporary ingredient. In honor of the traditional features, the brand logo is presented with Kanji calligraphy.

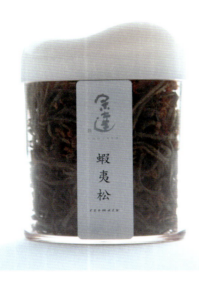

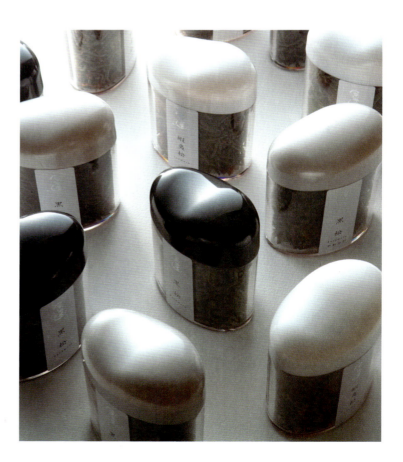

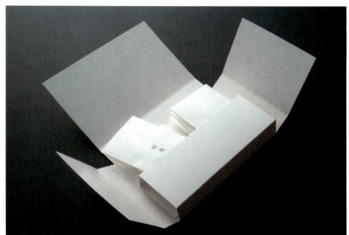

Designer: Ken Miki　Design Agency: Ken Miki & Associates

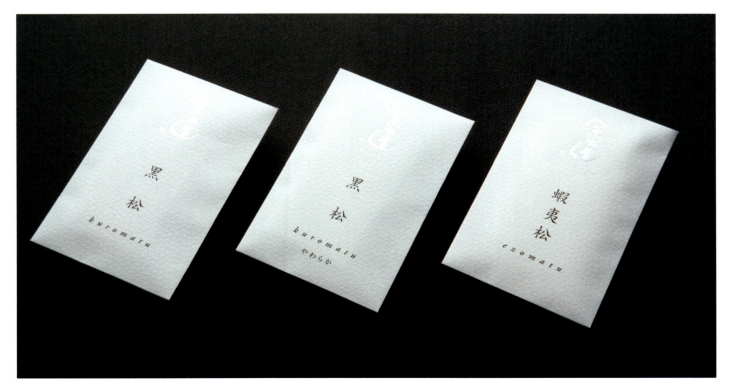

Chonmage Yokan

A chonmage is a topknot of hair, one of the most significant ornaments of the samurai, and Yookan is sweet bean jello often used as a gift. Chonmage Yookan combines these two traditional Japanese elements, resulting in an apologetic gift emblematic of a submissive retraction of honor, an act that is sure to smooth the nerves of any enraged wife.

Designer: Masahiro Minami

Tomato Juice

This label for tomato juice conveys its brand concept of "salt only," through minimalist packaging. To integrate the red of fresh tomato juice, and white, resembling, purified salt, the colors intermingle in the outer layer of packaging.

Designer: Junya kamada Studio: KD

Hontakachu Sake

Red-pepper flavored Hontakachu is a creation of local climate and culture. To present the relation between the floating red pepper and the liquor, the designer used a rectangle comprised of lines of letters. The whole packaging design showcases the relation between nature and human. Instead of Kanji, the text appears in Katakana, demonstrating the local characteristics of the product.

Designer: Jun Kuroyanagi

Ichirin

This project began with an environmental concept: reuse end materials. The bud vase, Ichirin, uses bamboo as its graphic motif. Accordingly, various design elements are developed from basic forms. The wooden box reuses a scaffolding board and can function as a gift or storage box.

Designers: Hajime Tsushima & Yukiko Tsushima Studio: Tsushima Design

Shiawase Banana

This product is environmentally friendly grown with organic fertilizers. Therefore, the designer decided to use banana-leaf-like boxes and packing material, applying banana-peel-like stickers to the surface of the banana. When the first layer of the sticker is peeled off, a story appears for customers to read.

Designer: Oki Sato　Studio: nendo

Nou No Mai

Rice is the main farmed crop of Japan. The mark on the packaging represents water, the sun, the Japanese flag and rice. The rice is grown by the farm workers with perseverance and dedication, the designer aimed to express this spirit by applying silk-screen printing over offset printing.

Designer: Kenichi Matsumoto　Studio: MOTOMOTO inc.

Warew

Warew, meaning Japanese Style, is a skin-care brand that carefully selects domestic and natural materials. A deep vermilion and pure white were chosen as brand colors to resemble a shiromuku, white dress kimono, worn when a women is perceived at her most beautiful, as a bride. This brand is derived from the uniquely Japanese aesthetic of wabi-sabi, which conveys the idea that beauty exists in simplicity and invisible spirit.

Designers: Eisuke Tachikawa & Takeshi Kawano Studio: NOSIGNER

Organic Fertilizer of Awaji Island

To convey the image of Awaji Island as a place whose residents raise livestock traditionally by plowing compost into the soil, the designer created the packaging to resemble the colors and textures of earth.

Designer: Yuka Tsuda　Studio: UMA/design farm

Loretta

Created for packaging an organic cosmetics line in accordance with the brand's image of innocence and playfulness, the designers combined the idea of plants bringing happiness to people with the wonder and friendliness of natural beauty.

Design Agency: Nippon Design Center

Norikko

This is a package design for Norikko, a dish made by the local women on the Seto Inland Sea of Ieshima. The dish consists of nori (dried seaweed) boiled in sweetened soy sauce. The black-and-white composition is designed to intuitively convey the notion of black Norikko on white rice.

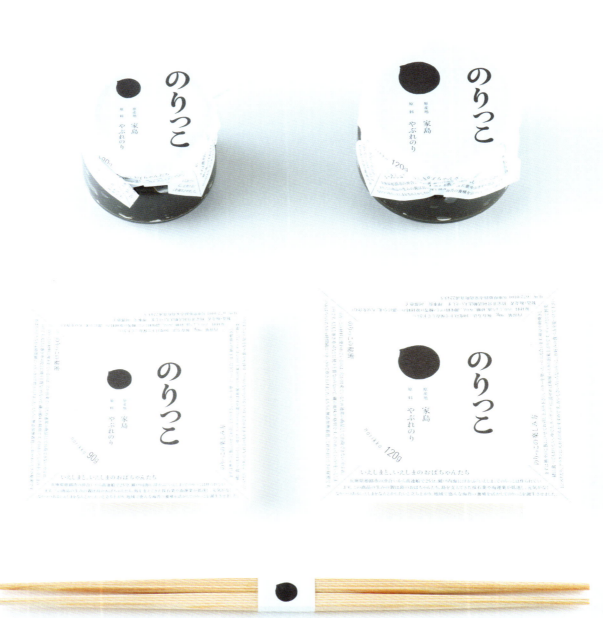

Quolofune

Quolofune is a confectionery company that, along with other sweets, mainly supplies Castella, originally from Portugal. The meaning of Quolofune is a black ship, and the design expresses this concept through simple and bold expressions on the package: mixed language logotype and the distinctive color contrast of black and white.

Designer: Shigeno Araki Design Agency: Shigeno Araki Design & Co.

Ine No Hana Sake

This old brewery announced a brand new product with four Japanese regional flowers printed on the wrapping paper, conveying a bold expression. The shape of the bottles reminds one of a Chochin, the beautiful and useful Japanese lantern, and also of an auspicious Daruma doll.

SIZUYAPAN

By using traditional Japanese family crests, this Sizuyapan design embodies the essence of Kyoto, a city strongly preserving traditional Japanese culture. Different varieties of anpan (sweet roll) have been designed, each with their own unique family crest, which reflect their characteristics.

MACCHA

CINNAMON

YUZU

MACCHA OGURA

OGURA

PLANE

ANNOIMO

SIRO

KUROMAME YUZU

SIZUYAPAN

SINCE 2012

Deli Cup

The studio was in charge of the design and packaging for Dialects Deli Cup and World's Thank-you Deli Cup, released by the Maruki Corporation Ltd. The whole design, especially the colors, convey a sense of vivid language.

Studio: G_GRAPHICS INC.

Arashiyama Chirin

Arashiyama Chirin is a driend whitebait store, intending to refresh its brand identity through targeting the young as its primary customers. Based on the new brand vision, the original food is developed into 16 different flavors, according to which SQUEEZE Inc. designed 16 types of package, each featuring different colors and patterns.

Setouchi Fruit Gelée

The designer was inspired by the seascape (Tadanoumi) when visiting the headquarters of Aohata, the brand's parent company. As a result, boxes bearing the image of the Seto Inland Sea came into being. Each package resembles an island, with trees of Lemon, Summer Tangerine, and Navel Orange.

Karakami Kit

Karakami is paper long used as decorative wallpaper inside traditional Japanese houses. The Karakami kit is a box containing everything necessary for printing personal patterns.

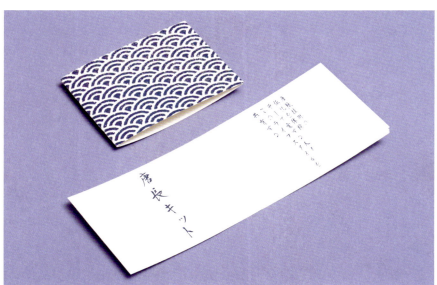

Designer: Jacopo Drago

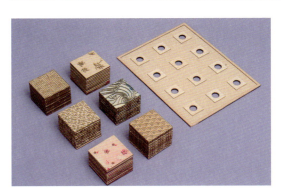

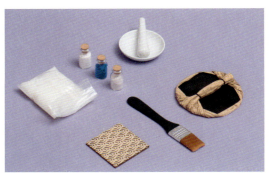

TOYOSU RAKUMIDO

Toyosu is the rice cakes manufacturer in business for 110 years, which is established in 1902. Rakumido is one of their popular brands for gifts. The designer created an imaginary flying bird pecking at the flowers and crops to communicate the brand's idea—Japanese blessings of nature in all four seasons.

とよす洛味堂
TOYOSU RAKUMIDO

Manga Plates

Each plate from the collection features various black-and-white drawings, which take on the personality of a frame from a manga anime. When food is arranged in a certain way on the plates, an animated visual is created. By placing these dishes in a particular manner you can transform your dinner table into a story, just like that of a page from a Japanese comic.

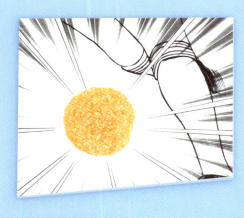

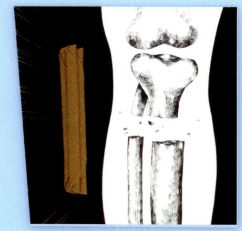

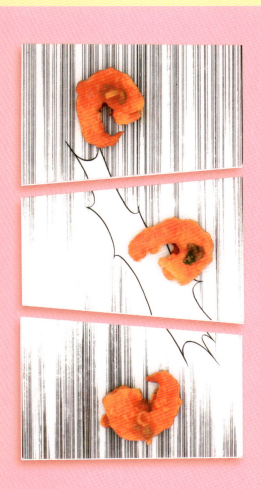

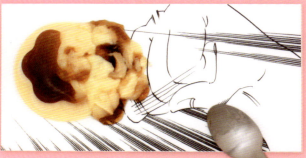

Designer: Mika Tsutai

Kokeshi Matches

Kumi had thought she would make something happy, using a matchbox, for a long time. Kumi started by drawing faces of KOKESHI, a traditional Japanese wooden doll: by hand, on each match. In 2000, Kokeshi Matches were mass-produced, and later featured different varieties, including chick and crane.

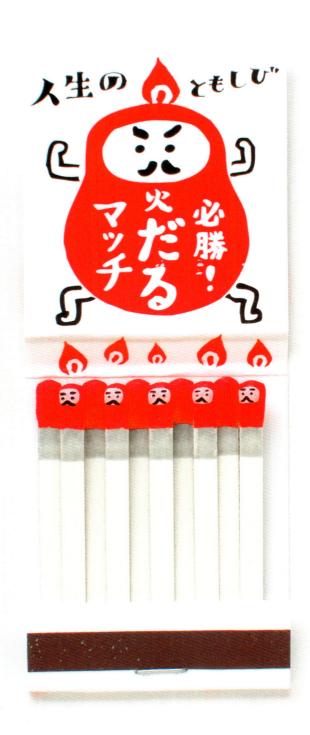

Designer: Kumi Hirasaka   Studio: Kokeshi Match Factory

Animal sumo OHAJIKI

This traditional confection gift box is designed with the goal of encouraging communication between friends and family. Apart from providing tasty confections, this gift box also gives people a moment of joy when playing with these animal figures.

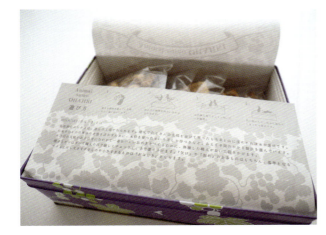

Dillii Cookies

This design was created for a fictional organic-cookie brand. The designer wanted mirthful packaging through humorous illustrations. Graphically, a red man with a burning tongue suggests a spicy flavor, whereas the astronaut's space green indicates a minty one. Most important, like cookies, the packaging means fun.

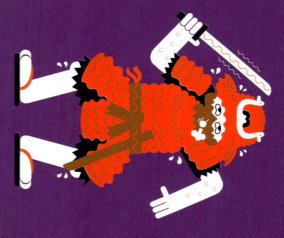

The Fishmen & Rice Wine

The art on this packaging is inspired by the fishery and brewery industries. To promote the Japanese town Setouchi, which boasts of a prosperous fishing industry, a fish image was chosen to portray a magical fish who can mysteriously brew the best sake in the seven seas.

Designer: Danis Sie   Studio: Sciencewerk

Small Sake

Packaging for most brands of sake looks more or less the same. To stand out, Small Sake fashioned small containers bearing modernized samurai patterns.

Designer: Nina Tahko Design Agency: Small Sake

Kenmin Box

These storage boxes provide souvenirs and gifts for tourists who enjoy collecting maps of Japan's provinces. Inside the boxes information and fun facts about the province delight and educate customers.

Studio: PORT

The Unclear Origins of the Mooncake Festival

Motivated by curiosity, the designer started to investigate the origins of the Mid-Autumn festival, aka the Moon Cake Festival. Although the origins remain mysterious and confusing, researching it was meaningful because it turned into a fascinating, creative process. In the end, the collected stories are illustrated on the moon cake packaging.

Studio: Tofu

Hitotubu Kanro

This packaging was designed for the well-known Japanese confection store located in the large Tokyo station. To meet the demands of tourists in increasingly great need of souvenirs and gifts, the design principles included handiness and cuteness.

Designer: Kazuya Iwanaga Studio: Draft

Magical Jammy

This product broadcasts its brand image as delicious, fun, and cute. In order to do so, each flavor was designed with an underlying theme. Pink stands for a love story between prince and princess, blue for a sunny-day picnic, and yellow for a joyful circus

Branding

Minimalism:
Minimum Expression, Maximum Impression

I believe design has been endowed with the ability to convey the meaning that words fail to convey.

Daigo Daikoku
| Art Director
| Daikoku Design Institute

Born in Hiroshima Prefecture in 1979. Graduated from Kanazawa College of Art in 2003. Worked for Hara Design Institute until establishing Daikoku Design Institute in 2011. Recipient of the JAGDA New Designer Award, the Tokyo ADC Prize and the D&AD Yellow Pencil Awards.

Good minimalist design work hides many things beneath its simple surfaces. Impelled by the most minimal of expressions, the viewer's imaginative space blossoms, leading to unfettered explorations deep within hidden worlds.

Design plays various and diversified roles in today's society. As a designer myself, I am involved in different fields such as graphic design, video, and space design, yet, I constantly remind myself to remain conscious of universality. One can display as many as 100 truths about something, but if they are not well communicated, a shadow will be cast on them, making it even more difficult to perceive clear images of their truths.

In a world full of differing values, to identify the essence among them and to hold tightly to it, is, I believe, of the greatest importance.

(1)

Being more than just a superficial visual communication technique, minimalist design is in fact an act to identify such an essence. In other words, minimalist design asks designers, relying on their own aesthetic sense, to boldly discard the excessive and secondary elements, and get to the really important elements.

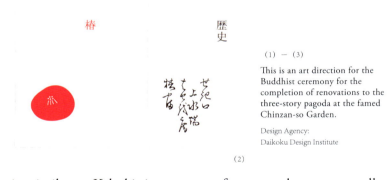

(1) — (3)
This is an art direction for the Buddhist ceremony for the completion of renovations to the three-story pagoda at the famed Chinzan-so Garden.

Design Agency:
Daikoku Design Institute

(2)

Noh, a classical Japanese musical drama that is quite similar to Kabuki, is a stage performance that removes all redundant elements and focuses on true aesthetics. Even in Japan, few people watch Noh performance. Once you do, however, you will find it alluring and fee; attracted by it. If you do not see through and try to understand those continuous subtle moves, you might find it boring. Just watch calmly for about 30 minutes, however. You will notice and experience its mystery and profound meaning in the tranquility you feel. From the delicate nuances of expression on Noh performers' faces, you can feel the entire range of human emotions. Then, the Noh stage becomes dynamic and fascinating. Viewers will make every effort to use their five senses to experience the subtle yet exciting changes in the air and then can realize how sensitive the five senses are. The heart is touched and shocked.

When the smallest change or element touches one the most, such experience becomes engraved in memory. In sensitive viewers, one subtle yet important element works magic: with few words needed. To put it in another way, curiosity can be triggered by a minute, insignificant element. This sensibility lies at the very base of Noh performance. Minimalist design in itself is the output of an aggregation of various energies and thoughts that aim to impress and touch the heart.

When it comes to the concept of intelligibility and clarity in design, there is often doubt in my heart. Minimalist art has long been established as a technique of artistic expression. In the design world, however, minimalist design is often seen merely as a superficial surface. Yet, beneath its simple and clear exterior lies a much deeper and more mysterious world. We tend to lose interest in knowing something further once we become too familiar with it. For example, since I was a child, I have been familiar with various drawings, films, photos, products, constructions, raw materials, characters, and so on. The reason they still hold my attention and attract me is their mystery. What remains unknown in them, which keeps inspiring me to learn more and to know further.

Japanese design is often regarded as the embodiment of minimalist design.

Japanese designers may not be aware that a work is minimalist, yet the world will place it within the minimalist category. Not all Japanese designers in all fields agree on that thought, though. This is probably because the Japanese look at design as an "expression" rather than a "solution." I also agree with this. What really matters is not the thought or the idea but whether a pleasant and fresh scene can come to life after the work is finished. I often remind myself to experiment and innovate, which, I think, is a duty entrusted to designers. In addition, I am always thinking of how to add dynamic designs in the graphic, three-dimensional, video, and space fields.

To know new things, of course, is important. But we also need to believe in the sense of the human body that is based on where we were brought up, the air and sunshine we have felt, and many things more. This sense brings resonance regardless of changing of eras or cultural background differences. A minimum of stimulation can lead people to dig more deeply into what is behind surfaces and to spontaneously capture the spirit and mystique of certain things, hence bringing happiness into daily life.

Minimalist design enables viewers to become proactive, a spirit that will have long-lasting influence on people's lives and behaviors.

> **Modern society is filled with easily accessible information. In contrast, simple representation may not be able to provide sufficient information, which could create concern or uneasiness to people who have gotten used to large amount of information. But at the same time, it grabs the essence and charm to win your heart in the blink of an eye.**

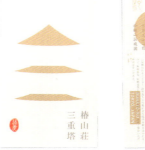 

(3)

GRAND MARBLE

The pine is a traditional Japanese image. To convey the historical brand identity, the designer merged the pine into every detail of the store, including packaging, logo, and decorative ornaments.

SOU·SOU

SOU·SOU is a Kyoto-born textile brand, making and selling a wide range of "things Japanese," such as Jika-Tabi (outdoor footware), kimono, furoshiki (wrapping cloth), and tenugui (hand towel). Sou-sou is a word Japanese frequently use in their conversations and can be loosely translated as "yeah, yeah," echoing another to show that "I agree with you." By integrating this idea into their design, the three founders are trying to reinterpret traditional Japanese culture and bring it back into people's daily lives.

SOU·SOU

Designers: Katsuji Wakisaka, Hisanobu Tsujimura, Takeshi Wakabayashi

Lisn

For several centuries, Shoyeido has been using natural ingredients (aromatic woods, herbs, spices, resins, and so on) to produce incense, which along with its traditional hand-blending process, contributes to the brand's longevity high quality.

Company: Shoyeido

Ninigi

In Japanese mythology, Ninigi, the son of Ame no Oshihomimi and grandson of Amaterasu, was sent to earth to plant rice. The designers merged this theme from Japanese mythology into the branding, where a combination of fishing-port feeling and Nó theater can be sensed.

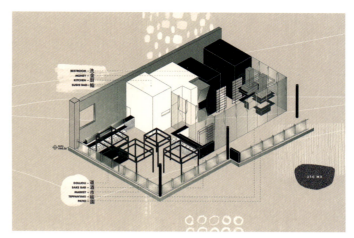

THE TRUE SPIRIT OF JAPAN

非常にクール

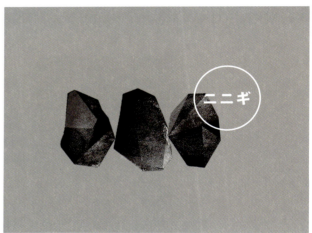

ニニギ

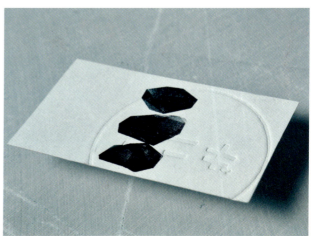

ニニギ 2014

書の箱りげるをよめる

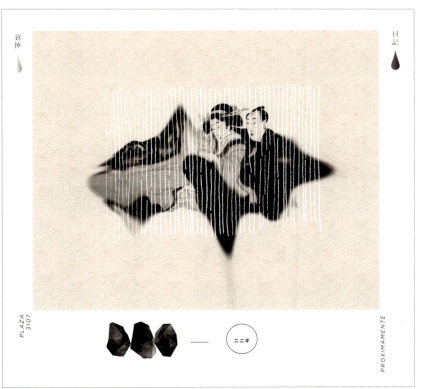

哀悼 日記

PLAZA
3107

PROXIMAMENTE

ニニギ

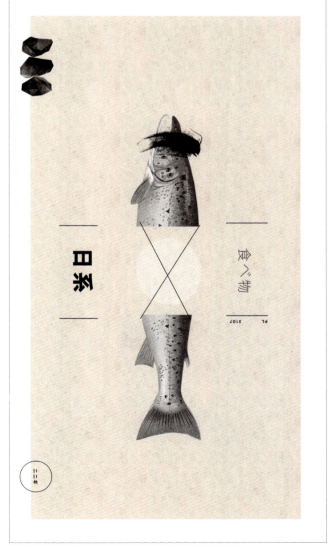

日系 食べ物

PL 3107

日本

The Three-Story Pagoda at Chinzan-so Garden

This is a publication for a Buddhist ceremony for the completion of renovations to the three-story pagoda at the famed Chinzan-so Garden. The communication tools were designed to remain consistent with the three-pagoda motif used for the ground-breaking ceremony the previous year.

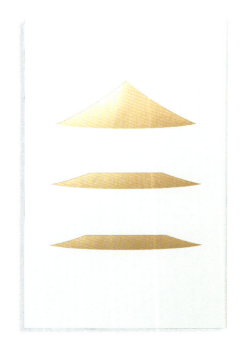

椿

歴史

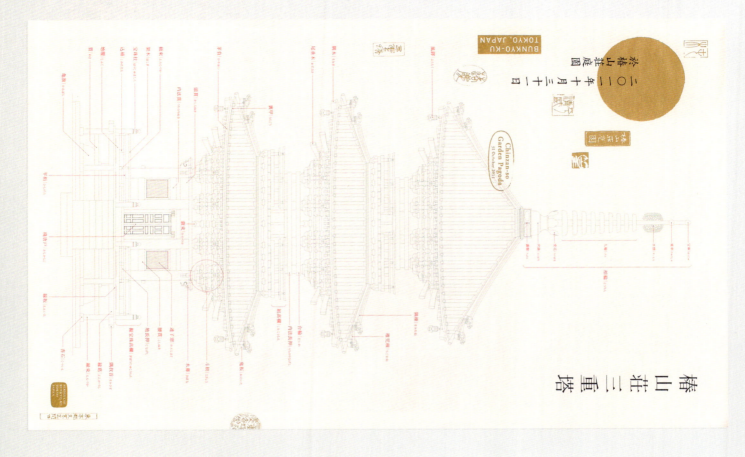

Hikeshi

Hikeshi is a high-end clothing line belonging to the Japanese brand Resquad. The general concept was inspired by firefighters of the 17 century, during the Edo period, in what is now Tokyo. They were considered to be as highly ranked as were samurai.

Oishii Kitchen Project

This design, by Cheng Li, is based on a mark depicting a mouth happy to have eaten something delicious. In a humorous way, this logo mark expresses the brand's worldview of "using the power of design for more delicious kitchens and dining."

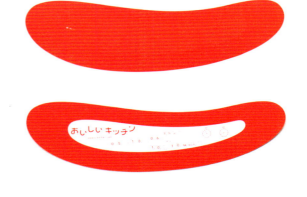

おいしい キッチン

Designer: Cheng Li   Studio: Nippon Design Center

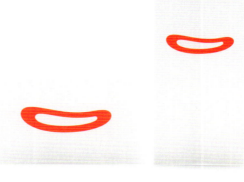

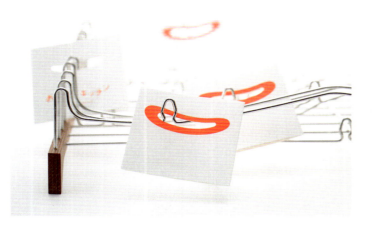

Mikita Apple Farm

To vividly present this apple brand, the designer playfully extracted the most essential element of the apple image—not the red color or the circular shape, but a few strokes suggesting a comic identity for an apple.

Designer: Junya kamada Studio: KD

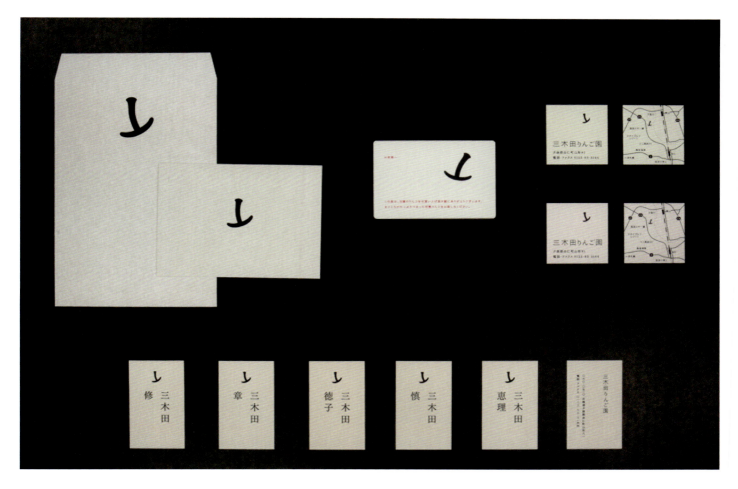

Super Normal Tofu

To design in accord with the historical image of tofu, the designer chose to use the furoshiki, a type of traditional Japanese wrapping cloth normally used to transport clothing, gifts, or other goods. The intention behind the design is to convey a sense of innocence and transparency.

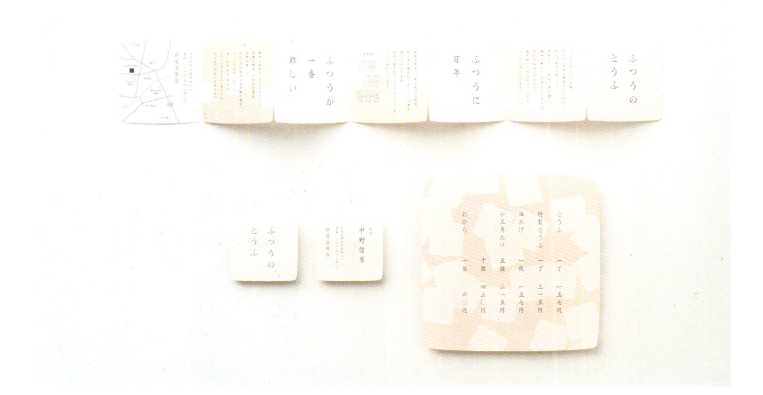

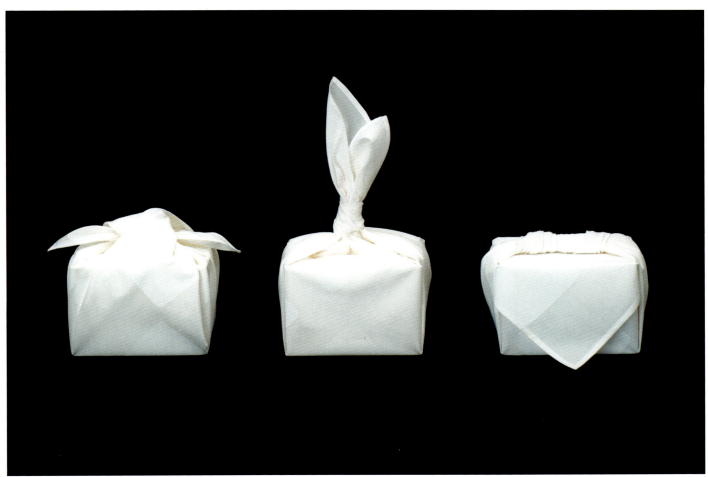

Designer: Junya Kamada & Atsumi Saito Studio: KD

Lacue

Historically, lettuce was found appropriate to grow in the hills. Lacue is a young company based in Kawakami, one of the largest lettuce-producing areas. The high altitude grants this area the vegetable's perfect growing climate.

Designers: Shogo Kishino & Miho Sakaki Studio: 6D

Micchan

Okonomiyaki is a Japanese savory pancake containing a variety of ingredients. Micchan Okonomiyaki is arguably Hiroshima's most famous okonomiyaki chain, which began selling the signature dish in 1950. To continue the established brand image yet refresh it a little was the designer's intention.

お好み焼
みっちゃん
井畝満夫の店
総本店

Stuido: IC4DESIGN

広島の復興とともに、生まれ育った味。

昭和二十五年創業。

み焼

ちゃん

井畝満夫の店

本店

広島の復興とともに、生まれ育った味。

昭和二十五年創業。

Shirokuma No Okome

This branding design combines the name of the brand, which means polar bear, with the brand's main product: rice. The designer transformed the tiny rice shape into the body of a polar bear, sometimes just the nose of the animal, giving customer an impression of cuteness and fun.

Designer: Ryuta Ishikawa　Studio: Frame inc.

The Big Ride

The Hong Kong Youth Arts Foundation was initiating a new project to promote cycling as a healthy and fun activity. Workshops were held to teach cycling tips to youth: road safety rules and basic bike repair skills. gardens&co. was invited to create the event identity, printed matter, and all promotional items used for these occasions.

w.hkyaf.com

@hkyaf.com

Designers: Kevin Ng, Wong Kin Chung & Jeffery Tam Studio: gardens&co.

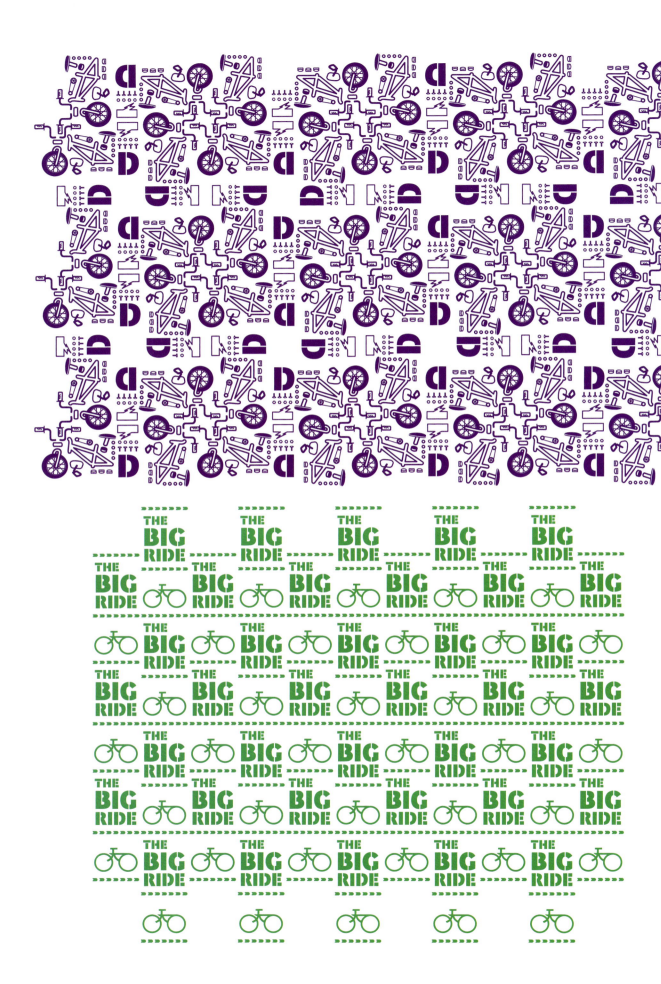

Origami Fun

Based on the design concept of "new buds sprouting on old trees," Cochae relates traditional Japanese folk toys, such as kokeshi dolls, Daruma dolls, and Kyoto characters, to origami. By injecting traditional characters into origami, people not only can enjoy the joy of folding paper, but also can appreciate the culture and tradition.

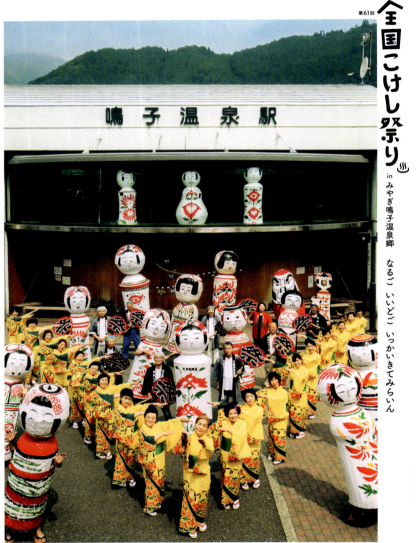

無限に顔が折れる
折りスジ加工付の紙のパズル!

FUNNY FACE

COCHAE
ORIGAMI PUZZLE

オリジナル ファニーフェイスカード　2種×各5枚　合計10枚入り　折りスジ入り　205mm×205mm
10papers / 5papers each 2types + diagram　The epoch-making origami puzzle with which a face breaks infinitely

ISETAN

MITSUKOSHI

Designers: Yosuke Jikuhara & Miki Takeda　Studio: Cochae

Komolabo

Komodaru, a kind of Japanese sake cask wrapped with straw mat, has been a heritage of traditional culture for proposing a toast, praying for health, happiness and auspicious beginning in congratulatory occasions. The idea behind this project is to maintain the traditional connotations while grant it a new image.

Poster & Book

A Brief Talk of Japanese Aesthetics

Ren Takaya
| Art Director / Designer
| AD&D

Born in Sendai, Miyagi prefecture, in 1976. Graduated from Tohoku University of Art & Design, majoring in sculpture in 1999. Joined good design company before establishing AD&D in 2011. I deal with graphic design and art direction. V.I. Received the Cannes Lions, Oneshow, D&AD, NY ADC, and NY TDC awards. Also The Brno Biennial Visitors' Award, the Hiiibrand Typography award, the JAGDA New Designer Award, the Japan Typography Annual Best Work Award and the Grand Prix, the Golden Bee 11 award, and others..

In a word, the beauty isn't just about the tangible substance; the Japanese world view and spirituality dwell in all senses of beauty.

Mono No Aware:

A concept coined by Motoori Norinaga in the 18th century, literally meaning "a sensitivity to things", is often use to describe the transitory nature of things. It suggests the experience of being deeply moved by emotions including joy, love, or even pain. The traditional love for cherry blossom is the most frequently cited example.

Minimalism rooted in history

The minimalism in graphic expression varies with the level of cultural maturity of a country. In the case of Japan, this minimalistic style originates from the historical context.

We can have a look at the works of the Rinpa and Kano schools. They are simple, and the their techniques of artistic expression, applied to present design elements in a limited space, represent the mind-set of Japanese culture. The technique of deforming the figures had hugely affected ukiyoe prints and paintings, which expressed manners and customs of the late Tokugawa period. I think it is strongly reflected in the field.

Feel the beauty through all senses

In general, people perceive Japanese symbols such as samurai, cherry blossoms, Mount Fuji, geishas, sushi, and so on. Indeed, they are the most obvious visual symbols of the beauty of Japan.

Yet, they are more than that: they are the aesthetic symbols of all the senses. Japanese people can feel beauty from the connotation and the scene indwelling each symbol. For instance, the light-pink cherry blossom is visually beautiful, but we can feel its beauty through other senses, too. Imagine the composition of the whole scene: the blue sky spreading over the cherry flowers, the black trunk of the tree, and the cherry blossoms whirling in the wind like falling snow. Blossom viewers feel the beauty of Sakura not only in the flower itself, but in the cozy breeze, the clear sky, the solid tree trunk. All of these add up to sensory and spiritual enjoyment. On the other hand, Japanese people always love cherry blossoms.

Handwriting, a way to think and believe

Ink, writing brushes, and Washi (Japanese papers) have been used as communication tools in Japan for a long time. For the Japanese, the spirituality inherent in Japanese calligraphy has always been of great importance.

When the Japanese want to express special feelings, they will write a letter, on paper, instead of typing on the computer. Because handwriting can embody trust and respect, which in branding design, the ink element is used frequently to some extent, especially in projects of historical brands in Japan, which are seeking to form an image of a long history and trustworthiness.

In modern times, the significance of design grow larger and larger throughout the globe, not only in Japan. Yet, compared with other industry, design haven't received enough attention. For every designer, it is important to help change the context and to create original works to provide solutions to the world.

Kamon, the inheritance of spirit

In the sense of a long history and trustworthiness, kamon a (Japanese family crest), contains the same connotation. It is one of the icons indicating Japanese-style tradition. Approximately 1,200 years ago, in the Heian era, the family crest came to be used in Japan as an emblem showing family lineage and the social status over time. Nowadays, it is not uncommon that kamon have been for the identities of shops, which pass on the kamon to the next owner. With its simple shape, there are plenty of variations. Many people still find charm in them. I think it is the reason why many Japanese designers use the family crest as one of the motifs.

The second president of LOUIS VUITTON, George Vuitton, once went to the Paris World Exposition, held in 1867. He was inspired by the Satsuma feudal clan and the kamon of the Tokugawas family, which participated in the Expo. He later designed the monogram of LOUIS VUITTON. All in all, family crest is an world-renowned example of the beauty of Japanese design.

Kamon — Japanese family emblems

Musashino Art University 2012

With the aim of emphasizing the role of the art university as a venue for creative activity, the message was condensed into the beauty of color, capturing the diverse potential of art's expressive activity in ovals with soft gradations.

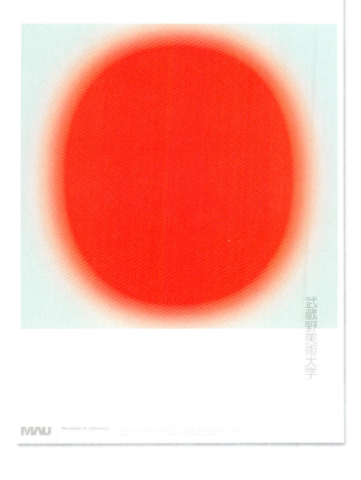

Designer: Takao Minamidate　Studio: Daikoku Design Institute

This is a poster design for THISWEEK, a music gathering about DJ music, aiming to present the combination of music, graphic, and image visually. The poster design incorporates simple geometric shapes embodying the name of this activity.

Shochiku Magazine Extra

Shochiku Magazine Extra is a special issue released on Shochiku's 120th anniversary of foundation. As the initial letter in Shochiku, "S" is used as a motif to express a kind of passion, motivation, and refreshing sense. The number 120 is designed to link the years 2014 and 2015, symbolizing the continuity and transition of time as well as a new vision towards a better year.

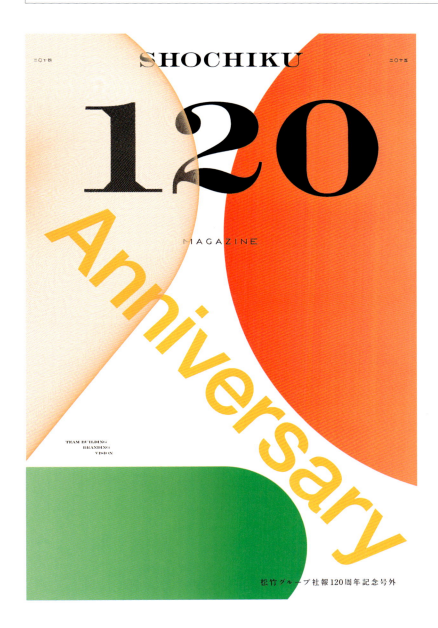

Designer: Motoi Shito

GEORGE NELSON Exhibition
-Architect, Writer, Designer, Educator

This project was designed for an exhibition held in the Meguro Museum of Art, Tokyo, with the theme of George Nelson, an architect, writer, designer, and educator. The poster design for this exhibition made good use of George Nelson's name by the seemingly random arrangement of its letters and of elements inspired by his most renowned works, such as the ball clock and the coconut chair. Bright red represents the color of Japan's of national flag, whereas beige conveys an antique feel.

Designers: Takeo Nakano, Kaoruko Naoi, Ami Kawase   Design Agency: Nakano Design Office

Ever since 2012, Yuri Uenishi has designed posters for the World Table Tennis Championships. The four posters, however, are quite different from each other, yet are all clear, unique, and aesthetically pleasing.

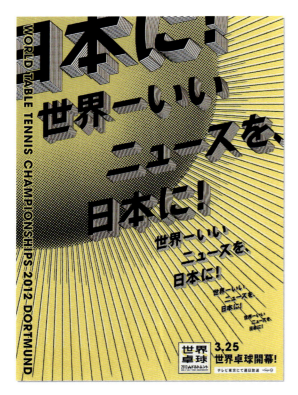

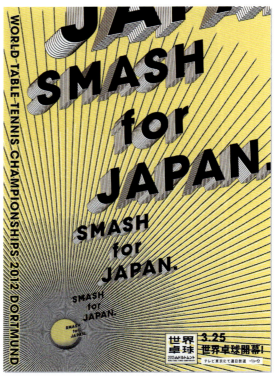

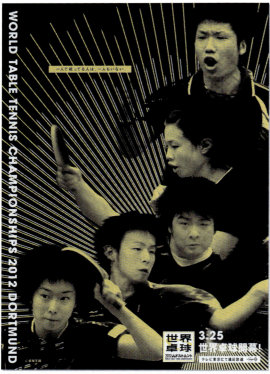

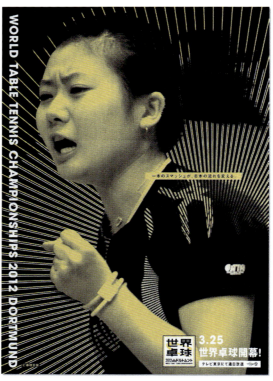

To portray table tennis's speed and momentum, in 2012, the designer used speed lines, often used in manga, to create a poster. The design was printed on golden paper to appear more attractive in the station.

In 2013 the designer collaborated with the famous Japanese manga, *The Ping Pong Club*. With the popular characters, the poster was a success and remembered by many.

Because Japan was the host country in 2014, Yuri Uenishi was especially aware of Japanese characteristics. The designer also collaborated with artist Taro Yamamoto, whose paintings featured traditional Japanese elements such as Mount Fuji, cranes, hanafuda (traditional Japanese playing cards), along with modern elements such as fences and airplanes. The poster portrayed Japan in a fresh way, using paintings and printing on holographic paper.

In 2015, the design was based on the theme of "the moment," trying to freeze the "so-fast-that it-seems-still" movement of sports. The designer had even ruled out the sense of space, featuring the intense moments when the winner might be decided.

2012

2013

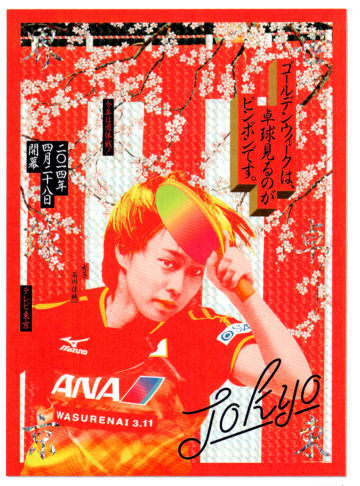

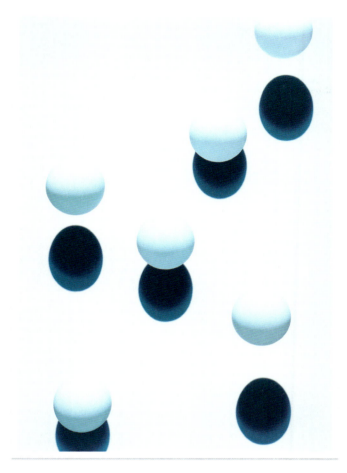

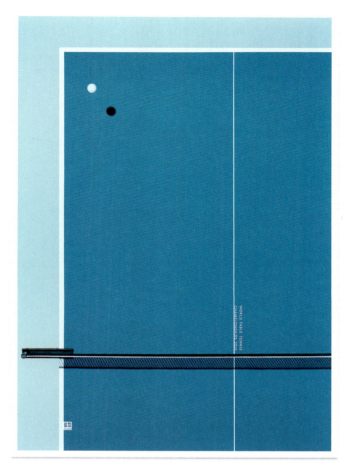

2015

JAGDA Junk Exhibition

This is a series of posters based on the theme of junk food, including Coca Cola, a hamburger, a slice of strawberry cake, and some French fries, donuts, and so forth. By deliberately omitting the details of these elements and using loosened strings, the designers created a carefree sense.

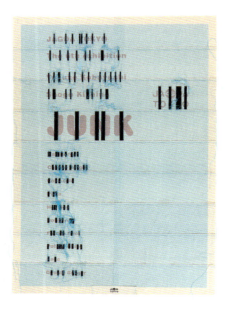

Designers: Shogo Kishino & Miho Sakaki   Studio: 6D

Nagoya Women's Marathon

The Nagoya Women's Marathon is the world's largest women's marathon, yet it is not that well known. So this poster is intended to demonstrate the sport's spirit by depicting the running postures of female runners and directly transmitting the event's features by using the Hanzi character "女", which means women.

ナゴヤには、
戦う女の物語がある。

女の都

New Year's Card Design

The 12 animal zodiac signs are important cultural symbols in China as well as in Asia, when people talk about calendars and the New Year. It is quite common for New Year's cards to depict the 12 animals of the zodiac as a main theme. The designer demonstrated a playful streak in reminding viewers of their comic book memories.

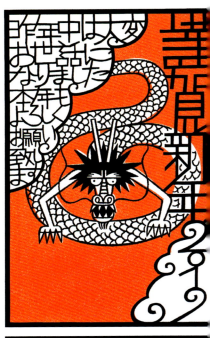

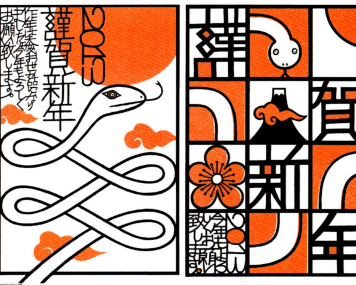

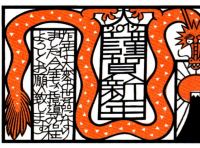

Design Agency: Studio-Takeu

Color and Shape

It is an experimental work that searched for the boundary of a practical visualization and an abstract image. The poster is printed with the offset printing. The card is printed by the letterpress.

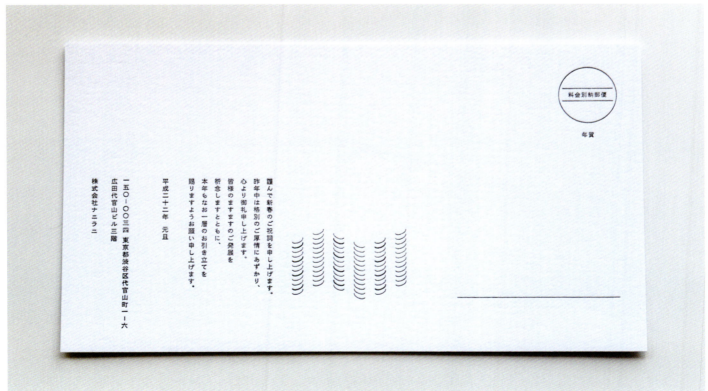

Designers: Keita Shimbo & Misaco Shimbo   Studio: smbetsmb

Books & Hats Party

The Books & Hats Party is a book-reading activity held by a handmade hat store, Viridian, and a second-hand bookstore, Rurodo. The two indie stores want to combine the two seemingly irrelevant objects. The poster took advantage of the element of hat and book as well as the English letter of Rurodo, conveying a feeling of ease and fun.

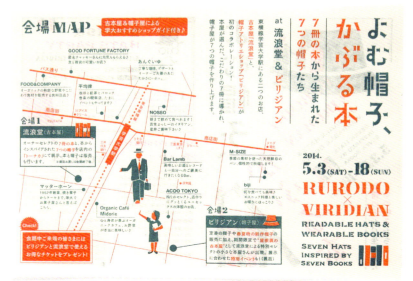

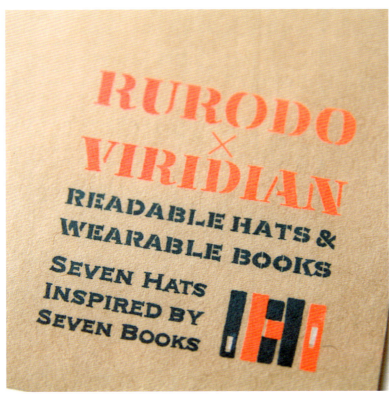

Studio: tegusu

This album cover design is for Japanese singer Remioromen. To depict the title of the album, Dream's Bud, flocking colorful birds appear as the motif.

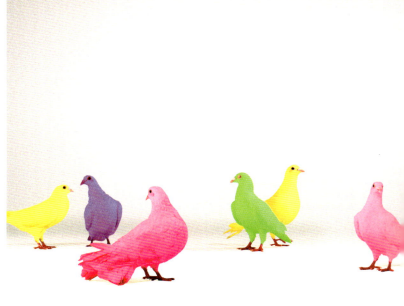

Designer: Atsushi Ihisguro Design Agency: Ouwn

Summer Class for Little Chefs

This promotion design is targeted to little kids and their parents. Therefore, this design took advantage of the cartoon images of a series of toys, such as sushi, plane, milkshake, pizza, hamburger and so on, to attract the attention of potential customers.

Designer: Wong Kin Chung Studio: gardens&co.

Cloud Font

Foregrounding one of the most classic of traditional Asian mythemes, auspicious clouds, this design's typeface flows cloudlike, following nature, asserting nothing.

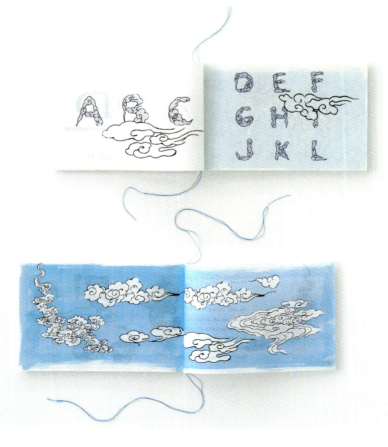

Designers: Shogo Kishino & Miho Sakaki   Studio: 6D

Bâtons, Chiffres et Lettres

In ancient times, people recorded numbers by using little branches, evolving gradually into mathematics, with literature evolving along with math. Inspired by this concept, this book strives to understand literature through numbers.

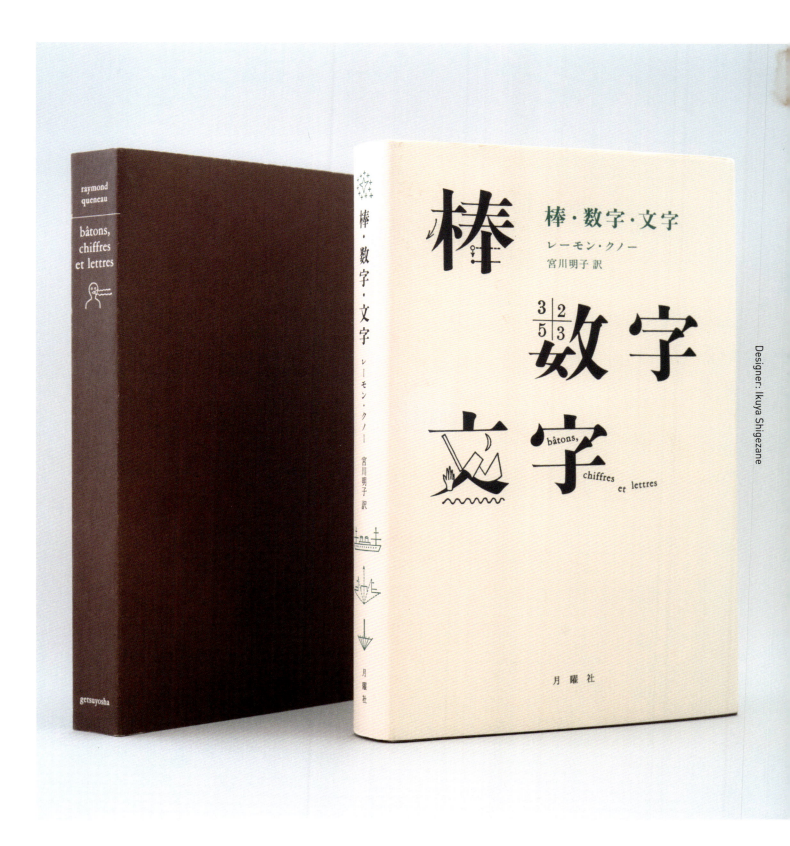

Logo Designs by Style

This book overflows with almost 1,000 Japanese-style logos, many based on stylized Hanzi. Thus, it provides an excellent source of ideas for designers interested in Japanese motifs and/or Chinese characters.

スタイル別 ロゴデザイン
Logo Designs by Style

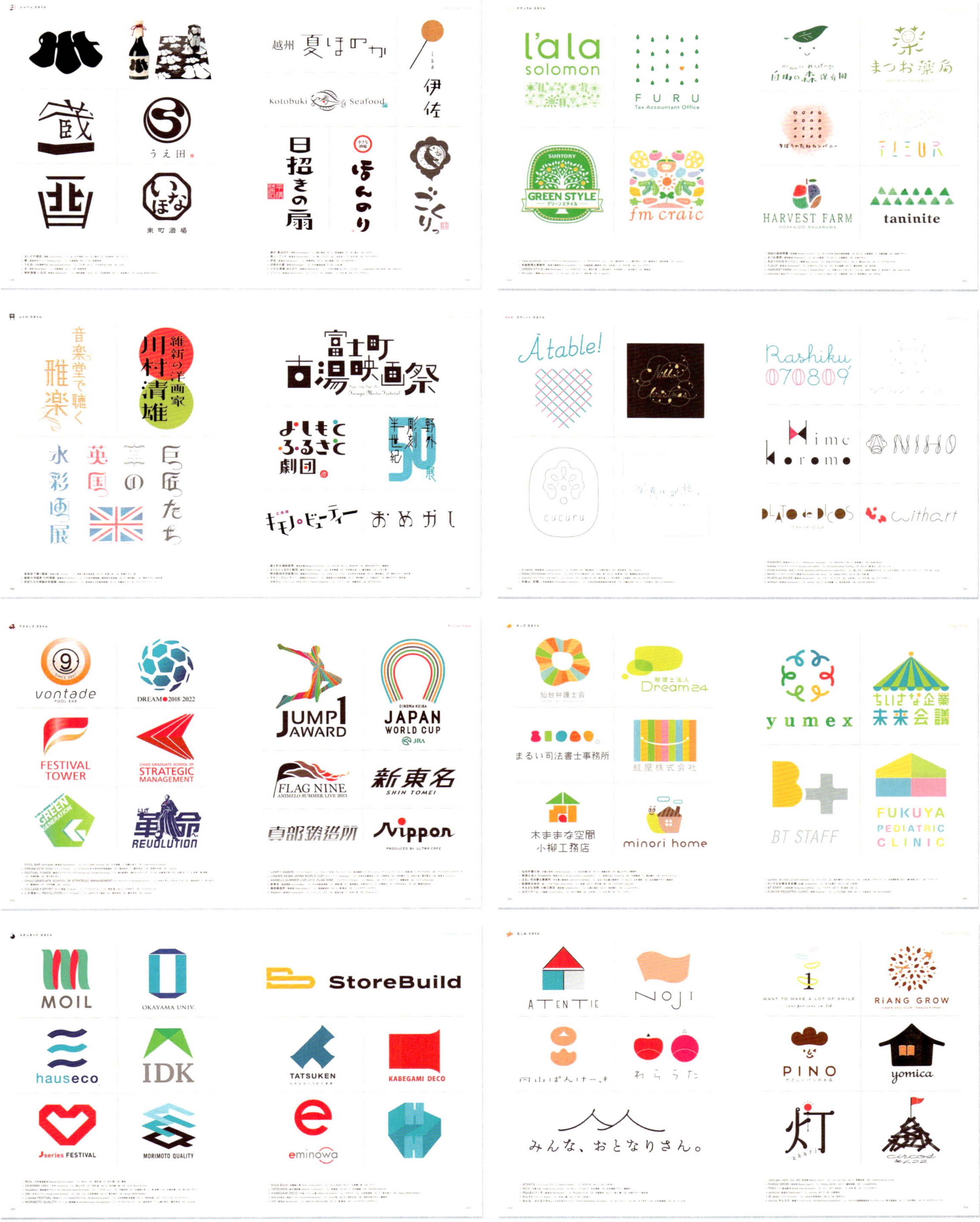

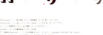

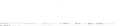

Publisher: PIE Books

The Four Seasons of Country Life

It is a collection of essays by the author on the subjects such as her relations with nature, harvesting of her produces and her cooking, in her reflections of her own country life in the changes of the seasons. The designer tried to express the implication of the title with abstract patterns of each season, applying them to the graphic motifs of the entire book, and to the typographies of the inside cover pages of "Spring", "Summer", "Autumn" and "Winter".

Designer: Masaomi Fujita　Studio: tegusu

Nostalgic printed matter
Museum of the family

This collection of Japanese graphic designs from the past 100 years is arranged to suit the perspectives of different family members. Accordingly, the cover features four portraits representing different ages and both genders.

Home of Raifuku

Inspired by this book's linguistic orientation, one of the book's lines referencing the main character ("I am Xu Xiao Xiao") is presented in four ways: Chinese characters, Pinyin, Japanese, and Taiwanese. The line suggests both Xiao Xiao's and the author's concern with self-identity.

Designer: Albert Cheng-Syun Tang Studio: ACST Design

The Anatomy of Evil

Because it raises deep issues about violence, psychological abuse, and forensic medicine, this book's cover features a blood-red color and ink-like strokes resembling blood stains—instantly communicating a suspenseful atmosphere.

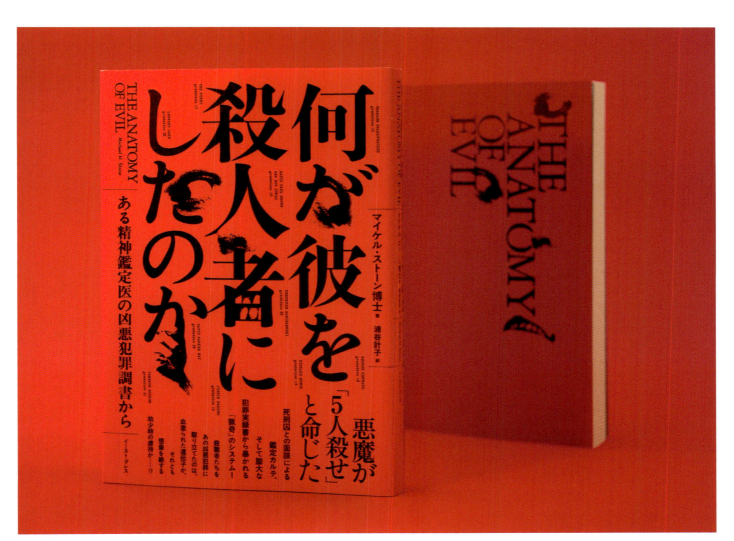

Designer: Ikuya Shigezane

Retrospective Medicine

This book collects Japanese medicine packaging and advertisements from the past 200 years. Titles of the book and chapters are designed with original typeface to convey a sense of humor and history.

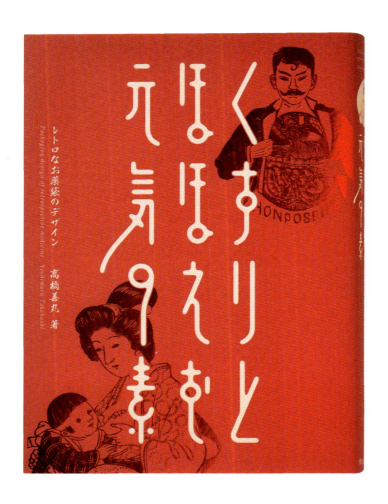

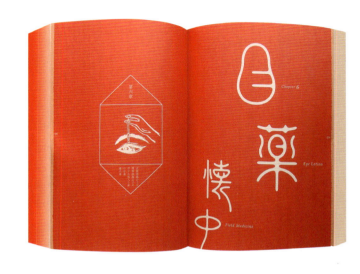

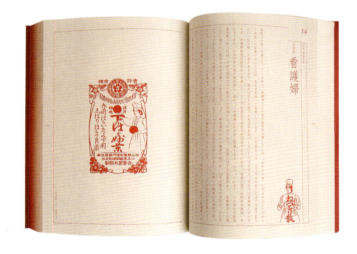

Race Against the Machine

This book cover's stark black-and-silver design strives to convey the threatening sense of metallic frigidity, helplessness, and unease humans feel when confronted by rapidly evolving machines designed to replace them.

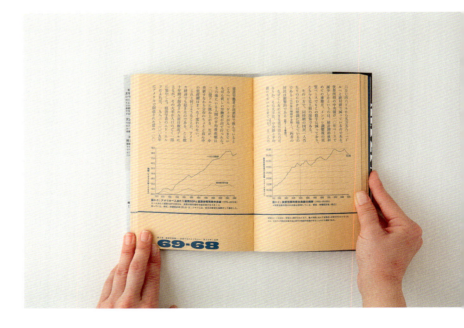

Designer: Asami Sato   Studio: Satosankai

Japanese Erotica

This book collects work from some of Japan's most popular contemporary artists. The works chosen depict the fringe Tanbi culture, in a Gothic mode, calling for black lace and gorgeous gold foil.

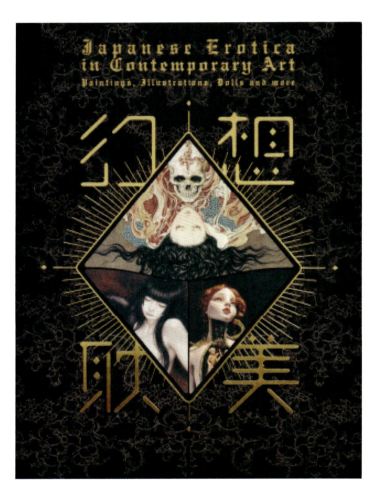

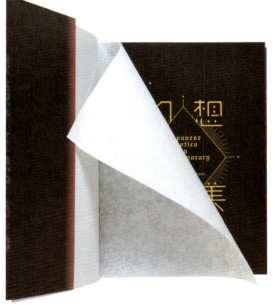

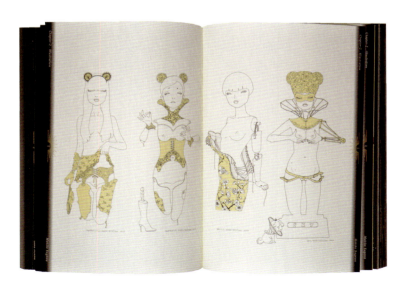

Designer: Yoshimaru Takahashi

Logo

What's the Nature of Japanese Graphic Design ?

When we look back on history, it is said that the Rinpa school, created 400 years ago and led by Koetsu Honami, established the foundations of Japanese design.

The Rinpa school is one of the major historical schools of Japanese painting and calligraphy. Its apparent characteristics lie in simple and dynamic composition, intensive use of negative space, and simplification of animals, humans, and nature. Throughout the world, the Fujin Raijin-zu (*Wind and Thunder Gods*) created by Sotatsu Tawaraya, is the most well-known masterpiece of this school. It is commonly known that Ikko Tanaka (1930–2002), the representative of Japanese graphic design, left with us numerous works that were influenced by the Rinpa school.

Masaomi Fujita
| Art Director
| tegusu

Masaomi Fujita was born in 1983 in Shizuoka Prefecture, Japan. After graduating from the Faculty of Design of Shizuoka University of Art and Culture, he engaged in planning, editing, and directing for several years. Reinventing himself as a designer, he worked in an advertising- production company and as a design and art director in the fields of cosmetics, fashion, and magazines. He established a design office, tegusu, in 2012, and now creates a wide variety of works—from concept planning to design work in CI and VI development—for corporate graphic and web designs.

Sotatsu began to work as a fan-painter in Kyoto. Later, he rose to work for the court as a producer of fine decorated papers for calligraphy. He was highly influenced by Kyoto's courtly culture and excelled in projects requiring meticulous placing of decorative screens and fans. He took this to its highest level.

Fujin Raijin-zu, early Edo period, two panels. National Treasure, Kyoto National Museum

Notable Rinpa artists:
Koetsu Honami
Sotatsu Tawaraya
Korin Ogata
Kenzan Ogata
Hoitsu Sakai
Sekka Kamisaka

Calligraphy of Poems from the 'Shin-Kokin Wakashu' on Paper Decorated with Deer

Decoration: Sotatsu Tawaraya, calligraphy: Koetsu Honami

Some traditional Japanese factors are also regarded as Japanese style, such as Japanese decorative patterns that are widely used in clothing and utensils, and Kamon (crest) which is used to identify family lineage. Even today, these factors are well cherished by designers.

The Japanese Imperial kamon—a stylized chrysanthemum blossom

the Prime Minister of Japan and Toyotomi Clan

Maruni Mitsu(ba) Aoi, the hollyhock crest of the Tokugawa clan

To go deeply into this topic, Japanese subcultures should be mentioned as well.

In recent years, promotional ads for games and animation; artwork, including album covers; and comic book covers have been of increasingly high quality. In addition, from album covers released by net labels and designs published by small media, such as ZINE and doujinshi, we are aware of a large quantity of experimental letterpress and abstract presentations that are not bound by market orientation. In practice, Japanese design as a whole is involved with pop culture, elements of American West Coast style, aspects of Parisian elegance and classic beauty, and so on. The orientation of design, however, has become more and more diversified. In other words, Japanese design is absorbing various influences and techniques—filtered, reconstructed, and applied flexibly by Japanese designers to meet with market needs.

For example, to activate regional vitality and encourage the inheritance of traditional craftsmanship and customs, people tend to resort to the power of design. There have been many similar cases in which designers have helped create packaging and promotion design by finding the links between a product and regional features. When I travel to the countryside, one thing I like to do is to find local artistic products. If you carefully observe the packaging, you will notice that reconstructions of traditional factors are involved. Japanese patterns such as Kamon, simplified images of natural imagery (such as Fujiyama, plum, and pine) are combined with a more modern palette, forms, and letterpress, imbuing these local products with original Japanese style. I think Japanese designers are all careful in handling the topic of how to represent their "Japanese nature," of proud leave their mark on traditional beauty.

Subculture:
In sociology and cultural studies, a subculture is a group of people within a culture who differentiate themselves from the parent culture to which it belongs, often maintaining some of its founding principles.

The Oxford English Dictionary defines a subculture as "a cultural group within a larger culture, often having beliefs or interests at variance with those of the larger culture."

What's the Nature of Japanese Graphic Design?

I think Japanese style isn't just about things that are featured with symbols of Japan. The true "nature" is the sensibility inherited from traditional beauty while being granted contemporary connotations, and the tenderness that comes from actively absorbing excellent ingredients from other countries as well as conforming to specific Japanese techniques of expression.

Chamcha

The brand of this Asian Dining Restaurant leaves an impression of a sun-tanned, wholesome, and delicate woman. To demonstrate the concept of gratitude for the blessings of nature, the logo was designed as a plate illustrated with three ingredients—sun, water, and flowers.

Designer: Naoto Kitaguchi   Studio: ANONIWA

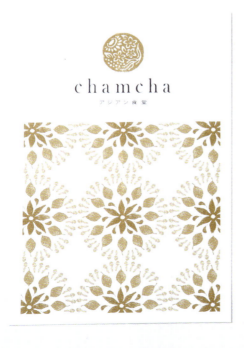

Maana Mikan Kihin

Kihin is known as the best quality brand among Maana oranges and is regarded as being in rank of its own. The brand designers emphasized the taste of the orange while appealing to a simple regionality of the production area. The whole design appears to be simple, yet the efforts become apparent in the details.

まあな
真穴みかん

薄皮 ㋻ 極甘

貴賓

Designers: Taku Satoh, Natsuko Fukuhara Design Agency: Taku Satoh Design Office Inc.

Kamata Nakarokugo

The design took inspiration from the resilient, hardworking swallow, in order to convey the image of a salon where you can soothe your fatigue and revitalize yourself. In addition, the designer also combined the swallow image with the Hanzi "力" meaning strength.

癒 処

蒲田仲六郷

relaxation

Studio: ANONIWA

Hagiwara Butcher

Hagiwara Butcher has been in business since 1947, in the ancient capital city of Kamakura. SPREAD designed a logo and a pattern that expresses the Chinese character for meat, which uses a motif of two roofs, one atop the other.

萩原精肉店

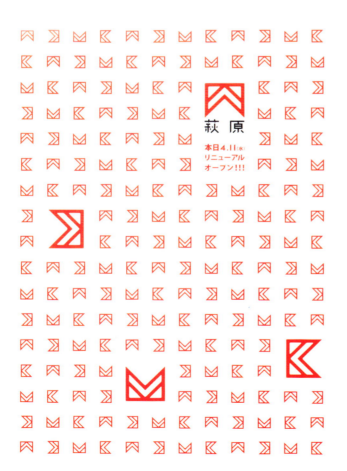

萩原精肉店

装いも新たに本日リニューアルオープン

オープン以来親しまれてきた町のお肉屋さんが、おしゃれな鎌倉のお肉屋さんに変身
これからも末長く愛されることを願い、スタッフ一同皆様のご来店を心からお待ちしております

リニューアル記念セール開催 (100gあたりの価格です) セール期間 4／11・12・13・14

Designers: Hirokazu Kobayashi, Haruna Yamada, Satoko Manabe　Design Agency: SPREAD

萩原精肉店

営業時間 9:30 ▶ 18:00　定休日 日曜・祝日
〒248-0006 神奈川県鎌倉市小町1-4-29
tel & fax : 0467-22-1939
www.kamakura-shops.com

Miso

This project was developed for a contest: Roooots Setouchi Specialty Products Redesign Project 2013, Tokyo, Japan. Miso is a traditional Japanese seasoning produced by fermenting rice. The logo was designed in black, white, and red, corresponding the three types of miso produced by means of different lengths of fermenting time.

にんにくいりこ味噌

Miso Spread with Garlic & Dried Sardines

Kakino Kinoshita

Kakino-kinoshita is an art gallery transformed from an 80-year-old folk house. For the house, designer developed a gallery logo based on traditional Japanese family crests that represent family trees and pedigrees. The design has been expanded into multiple versions using the traditional Japanese color scheme and a persimmon-calyx background pattern was created.

Kakino
Kinoshita

Kakino
Kinoshita

50mm

35mm

25mm

18mm

11mm

Top view of Persimmon

Graphic Pattern Motif

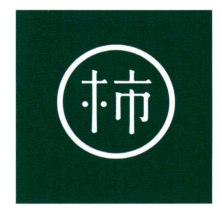

Dark Green／深緑　ふかみどり
C:100% M:15% Y:70% K:50%

Rose madder／茜色　あかねいろ
C:0% M:90% Y:75% K:28%

checkerboard pattern／市松模様

Designer: Masaomi Fujita Studio: tegusu

Ayumi Kinoko

Ayumi Kinoko is a brand of Juda's ear mushroom cultivated in the Amakusa region of Kyushu. As a cooking ingredient, Juda's ear is unfamiliar to many. Thus creating a new image for Juda's ear, the designers used a fungus motif, lending the vegetable a more recognizable allure.

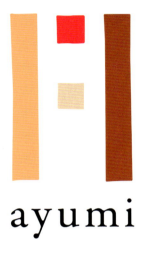

ayumi

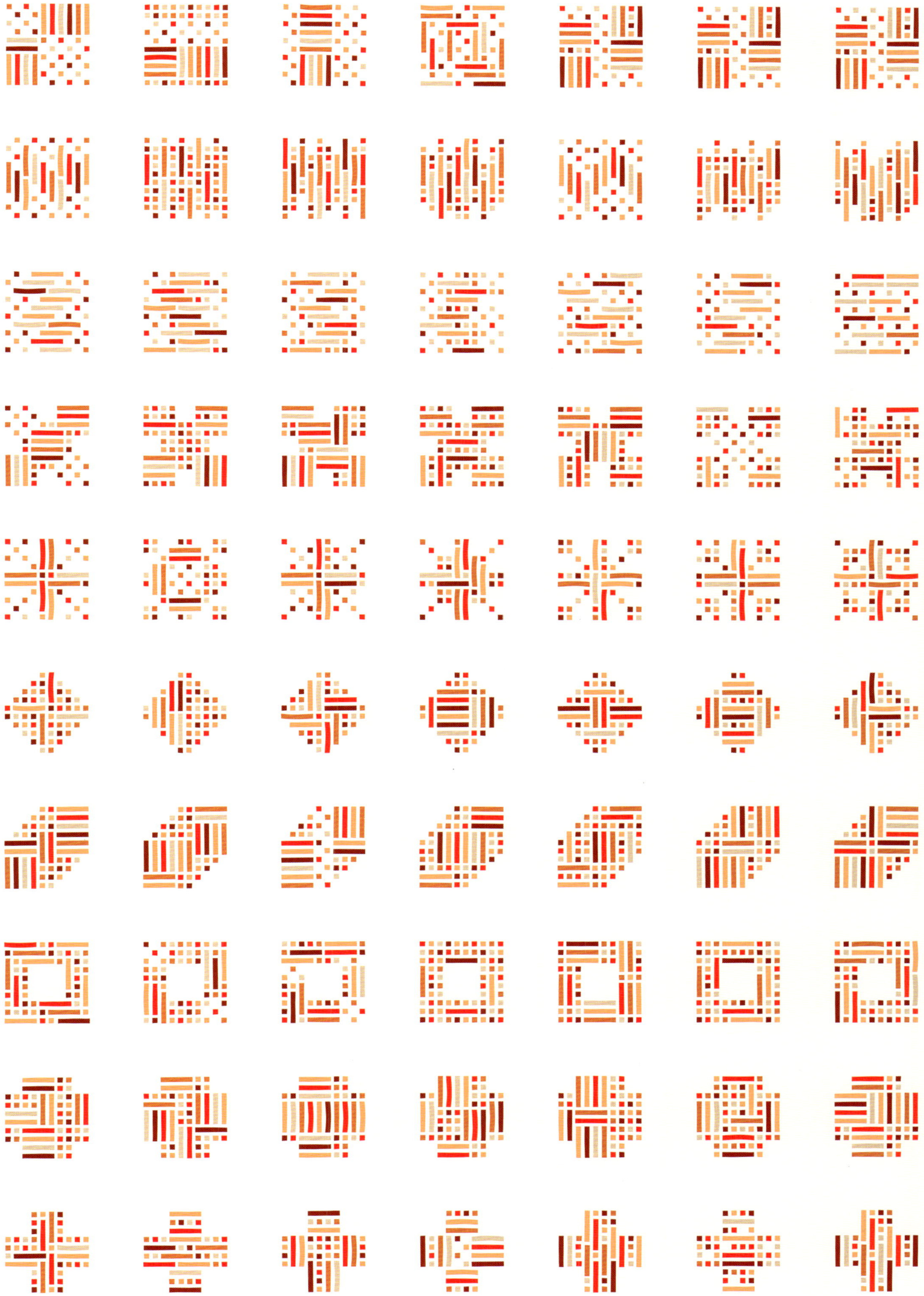

Design Agency: canaria

Kyoto Nakasei

Kyoto Nakasei is Japan's pioneer of dry-aged beef. The new logo features a circle with a single line through the center, emulating the character " 中 ". used in the shop's name and expressing the owner's credo: "bringing cow, people, and meat together." The wine-red of dry-aged beef is used as the brand color, enhancing the connection of identity with product.

京都
中
勢
以

Design Agency: canaria

Horitaro HSRG Tattoo Studio

Koi is a highly respected and strong Japanese symbol often used in traditional tattoos. The designer chose only two colors in addition to the paper's white: black, referring to the black ink and vermillion, a color used extensively in Japan, in places such as Shinto shrines or on lacquered tableware. The tattooist nickname, in Kanji, has been printed in letterpress, and the studio name is treated like a stamp.

Momonoki

Momonoki, meaning peach tree in Japanese, is a renewal Chinese restaurant. 6D strived to present the brand image as vigorous and young while maintaining the quiet character of Japanese style.

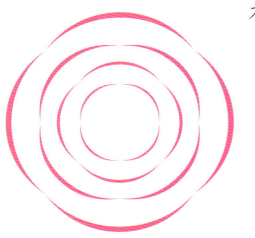

Designers: Shogo Kishino & Miho Sakaki Studio: 6D

Ippon Matsu Beer

This beer's name means One Pine Tree and its design is a symbol of charity and hope for Japan's future. A scroll-like, handwritten label seals the top with its message, written on the inside. The label depicts a solitary pine made of three triangles facing upward, symbolizing the wish for reconstruction in the aftermath of tsunami of 2011.

Designer: Kota Kobayashi

Shinajina 7th Anniversary Card

Shinajina is a bonsai shop in Tokyo. This greeting card commemorates the seventh anniversary of the shop. The character is letterpress, and the moss ball were taken in the photograph is silver leaf.

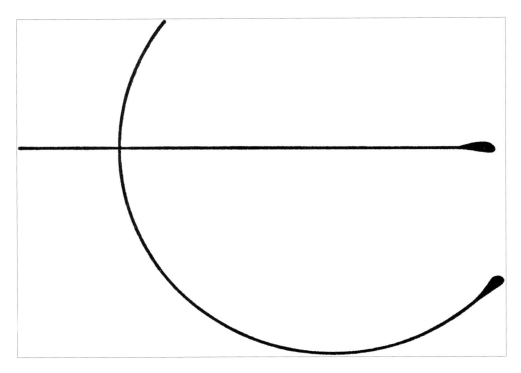

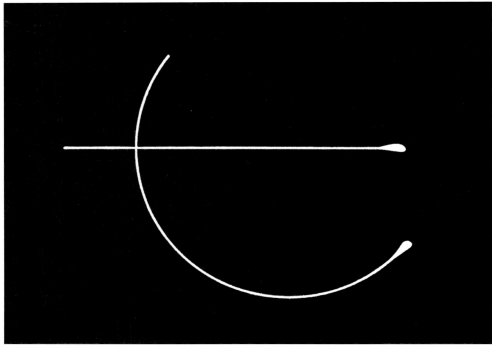

Designers: Keita Shimbo & Misaco Shimbo Studio: smbetsmb

Morishita Music School

Morishita Music School promotes a learning method of using various musical instruments and body movements. The designer took an inspiration from a German folk song, "Ich bin ein Musikant" which is well known in Japan as "Animal Musicians of forest", so a design of animals playing instruments was created.

もりした音楽教室

Morishita Music School

もりした音楽教室
静岡県藤枝市光洋台
〒126-0079
電話 090-1749
メール (agmail.com)
ブログ ameblo.jp ms.morishita

Designer: Masaomi Fujita Studio: tegusu

The logo for roost resembles a bird's nest. The logo suggests that the hair salon will be a place where customers can feel relaxed, at home, and eager to return. The logo also embodies another message that roost customers will be filled with new hope and fly away into the future on the wings of their new hair style.

roost
warmly hair

warmly hair
roest

Hair Cut, Hair Color, Perm,
Straight Perm, Treatment, Head Spa,
Facial, Hand Massage,
Hair Set, Makeup, etc..

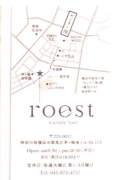

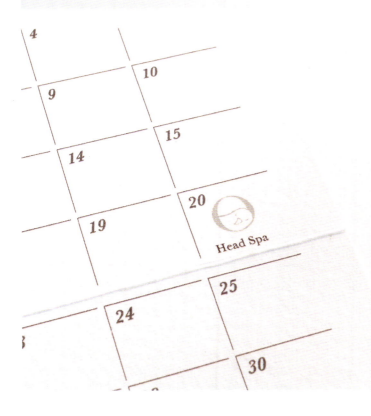

Designer: Masaomi Fujita Studio: tegusu

Puzzle Gakuen

Puzzle Gakuen is an educational service using intellectual training materials. As a motif, the designer created a logo with infinitely changeable possibilities, just like a child's power of imagination when using tangram, one of those teaching materials.

Desginer: Masaomi Fujita Studio: tegusu

This logo mark used one string to draw out the name of the brand, while maintaining a basic horizontal line to resemble the horizontal line of the earth with building constructed on it. In this way, the architect characteristic of the brand is implied.

Kawashima

mayumi

architects

Designers: Shogo Kishino & Miho Sakaki Studio: 6D

Viridian - 2015 Spring/Summer visual

This is a 2015 spring&summer season visual for Viridian handmade hats. New hats were inspired by an old film, *Funny Face*, starring Audrey Hepburn. The designer portrayed the musical scene in the center of Paris via springy typography.

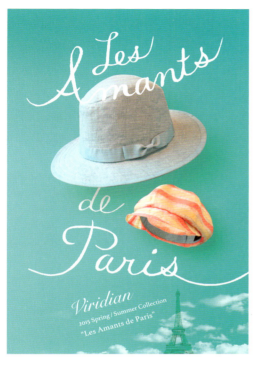

Desginer: Masaomi Fujita Studio: tegusu

INDEX

ACKNOWLEDGEMENTS

We would like to thank all the designers and contributors who have been involved in the production of this book; their contributions have been indispensable to its creation. We would also like to express our gratitude to all the producers for their invaluable opinions and assistance throughout this project. And to the many others whose names are not credited but have made helpful suggestions, we thank you for your continuous support.

FUTURE PARTNERSHIPS:
If you wish to participate in SendPoints' future projects and publications, please send your website or portfolio to editor01@sendpoints.cn.